VOLUME I

UNLOCK TECHNOLOGY WITH THE COMPUTER PUPPETS FOR GRADES 3RD–5TH

Rene' Compton

Additional Resources Available with book purchase
- Game Board Components Free download at www.computerpuppets.com
- 4-Part Video Production Free download at www.computerpuppets.com
- Two Technology Adventure books
  1) Rainbow Pixel of Hope
  2) Computer Pirate

Achieve the ISTE standards in technology literacy and have fun doing it with the Computer Puppets!

ACKNOWLEDGEMENTS

I dedicate this book to God for always giving me hope and determination to never give up on the Computer Puppets Project. I praise him for providing the wisdom to write the instruction, stories and produce the video production. Without him the Computer Puppets would not have been created. It has been an amazing journey with God. I feel very thankful to be a part of it all, even in the valleys. Each time I thought of giving up he would always be there to give me new inspiration and set me upon a mountain of hope. I pray that you will enjoy teaching and learning with the Computer Puppets and that it will give you inspiration to do whatever God has called you to do. I encourage you all to not BELIEVE in yourself but in GOD that is within your heart and soul.

I would like to thank some very special people that God sent to help on this 12 year mission.

First, I would like to thank my husband and best friend which worked hard while I tried to breathe life into each puppet character. I love you...

Thank you to both my sons and SBB's, Ryan and Spencer who made Computer Puppets, Chip and Ram come to life. To hear their voices on the video production always made the project worthwhile. I love you both so very much.

Thank you to my dear friend Nancy Vlasaty who spent hours editing the manuals and stories. You always made it better!

Thank you to my dear friend Hildegarde Staninger who always encouraged me to believe in the mission that God had given me and to never give up.

Thank you to my dear sweet Daddy and my Sister who inspired me with their entrepreneurial spirit. Daddy always taught us both to dream and reach for the sky!

Last, but not least I would like to thank my dear and precious Grandmother, Ethel Priest for being my inspiration and spiritual foundation. You set the example of what a true Christian should be! What a blessing you have been in my life. A true angel on earth!

My favorite Bible verse, which keeps me encouraged is Romans 8:28.
And we know that all things work together for good to them that love God, to them who are the called according to his purpose. KJV

The Computer Puppets is a proven innovative approach for teaching that enables students and teachers to embrace their world of computer technology. These puppets in conjunction with our Learning System help students of all ages comprehend abstract concepts, develop a robust level of computer understanding, and provide numerous meaningful learning experiences. Our in-depth Learning System establishes a solid foundation beginning with computer elements and components coming to life for the students as probing, adventurous puppets. All can relate to The Computer Puppets as fundamentals are explored through their escapades. Commonly felt inhibitions and frustrations melt away when students are brought into the fascinating world while developing essential skills for today's education.

3 – 5th Grade – Part I – The Missing Computer Component

> **IMPORTANT REMINDER TO STUDENTS AND STAFF!**
> **NEVER, NEVER WITHOUT TRAINED TECHNICIAN OR SUPERVISION**
> **GO INSIDE THE COMPUTER HOME! OR COMPONENTS'**
> We never look inside the computer because of the danger of being shocked
> by electricity. Even when the computer is not connected to an electrical
> outlet the Power Supply inside the computer holds electricity.

Duration

This unit is completed over a three–week period; it should be integrated into your normal computer classroom.

Computer Lab – You may wish to have classroom teacher provide coloring activity. Discussion of cut and paste projects are suggested within the computer lab.

Objectives

- Provide students with the understanding skills of the basic hardware
- Introduce the students to components and basic troubleshooting skills

Learning Outcomes

At the end of this unit, students should:

- Be familiar with CHIP, RAM, ROM and Motherboard
- Be capable of locating them on the coloring page or classroom computer model
- Understand the importance of closing out programs before powering off
- Have acquired basic Troubleshooting skills

Format of Learning Activities

- Classroom activities – enclosed packet for Part I – The Missing Computer Component
- Video review of Part I
- Classroom discussion with questions and answers (Flashcards)

Part I

The three 20-minute classroom lesson plans, detailed below, provide students with an introduction of actual computer components. They will be introduced to technical terms and given time to interact with and enjoy The Computer Puppets. This part will emphasize how important RAM is to the computer and to programs. It will also encourage students to think of how the computer works from the inside out.

LESSON 1: Resource Folder and My Home Design Project

<u>**Preparation and materials**</u>

- ✓ Provide folder for each student for Resource Folder
- ✓ Have a blank diskette for each student for My Home Design Project if printer is not available – This activity can be drawn on paper and achieve same results with understanding and relating to computer
- ✓ Bring from class or provide colored pencils for My Home Design Project

Resource Folder
- ❑ Have students decorate a folder with pockets and prongs to keep as a computer resource folder. Please have students keep all information within this notebook and use it as a resource for computer lab and classroom all year.

My Home Design Project
- ❑ Provide a blank diskette for each student <u>if printer is not available</u>.
- ❑ Ask students to draw a picture of their home with a paint accessories program. (Click START - PROGRAMS - ACCESSORIES - PAINT)
- ❑ Request placement of circles for individual family members who live within their homes. Put these members in their favorite places.
- ❑ Brief discussion about their rooms and places where they keep their things. (This can be discussed while creating document to save time.)
- ❑ Save document on diskette, inserting diskette into small drive - A: Drive. Then click: File - Save As. Arrow down on Save in: and select A: 3½ Floppy Drive.
- ❑ Skip saving work if printer option is available and proceed with clicking onto File - Print.

LESSON 2: My Computer and Video

Preparation and materials

- ✓ Provide colored pencils and scissors for class
- ✓ 1 envelope for each student in classroom
- ✓ Provide each student with Worksheet 1 (My Computer)
- ✓ Have available CHIP and RAM Puppets
- ✓ Video – Part I – The Missing Computer Component

- ❏ Provide each student with a copy of Worksheet 1, MY COMPUTER, and request they color components with the colors shown.
- ❏ Show the class CHIP and RAM Puppets and allow interaction with actual puppets.
- ❏ Play the VHS Video – Part I – The Missing Computer Component (approximately 12–minute Video)
- ❏ After video, request that students look at My Computer coloring activity – remind them of Programmer's Lab in the video and Puppetizer 3000. Request they cut out computer component/parts only not words, place in envelope provided, and place in their resource folder! (Note: Cut appropriate places shown on My Computer – This could require some assistance.) DO NOT GLUE YET!

LESSON 3 – Name that Component

Preparation and Materials

- ✓ Worksheet 1 – My Computer
- ✓ Envelopes with cutout components (students should have these in their resource folder)
- ✓ Notebook paper for Resource Folder
- ✓ Provide glue for classroom us
- ✓ Worksheets: 2 – CHIP, 3 – RAM, 4 – ROM, and 5 – Motherboard (Recommend that instructor/teacher color a copy of worksheets 2–5 which will be used as flashcards for class discussion and quizzing.)

- ❏ Review instructor/teacher flashcards of "The Before and After Components" – CHIP, RAM, ROM and Motherboard.
- ❏ As each component is reviewed on flashcards have students glue the appropriate component in its proper place in My Computer drawing (Teacher Activity & Answer Guide is provided).

- When all components are glued, fold My Computer worksheet along centerline as shown. This will make an excellent reference for students and should be kept on display or in resource folder for reference while proceeding through "The Computer Puppets Learning System".
- Request that students identify each component that was discussed in the video and proceed with coloring the Worksheets 2-5.
- <u>Write the following questions</u> on the board and have students answer on a sheet of notebook paper and put in resource folder without looking at the worksheets on "The Before and After Components" flashcards.
  - <u>Who is RAM?</u> - Random Access Memory - He is the Big Cheese. You need him to run the fun games on the computer.

  - <u>Who is ROM?</u> - CD ROM is where the fun games are put in the computer. You always close (X) all the programs on your screen before taking ROM from his home. Blue screen reminder!

  - <u>Who is CHIP?</u> - Computer Chips are how the information is stored in the computer; these are electrical currents. REMINDER - We never ever look inside the computer because of the danger of being shocked by electricity. Even when the computer is off, the Power supply inside the computer holds electricity.

  - <u>Who is MOTHERBOARD?</u> - She holds all the components. Remind students that she is the backbone of the operation! Make a comparison of their mother to motherboard and stressing how protective a mother is. You can also point out that a Motherboard is very delicate.

  - Hard Drive - Is our "Mystery Component" and will be explained in a later video. Wonder who lives inside the Hard Drive. You will find out in Part III, "Somebody Help! Call the Doctor!"

Teacher alert! - Watch for a **Brain Wave** shown on "Name that Component" flashcards.

Evaluation

Students should be capable of identifying the components:

- ❑ Journal or verbal reflection on what they learned in each of the activities. (I know, I think, I wonder – One sentence on each of these about the computer. The responses can show the teacher what the students are still unclear on.)
- ❑ Participation in the classroom activities
- ❑ Have the students display Lesson 1 – My Home Design Project and My Computer in the classroom or hallway.
- ❑ Children should be familiar with where to find the amount of RAM in a computer

Where to go from here

After confirmation of understanding of basic components, proceed with Part II – Code's Search for More Memory – Lesson 4. Lesson 4 will reinforce the introduction to components/hardware and will be an insight to programming and different languages.

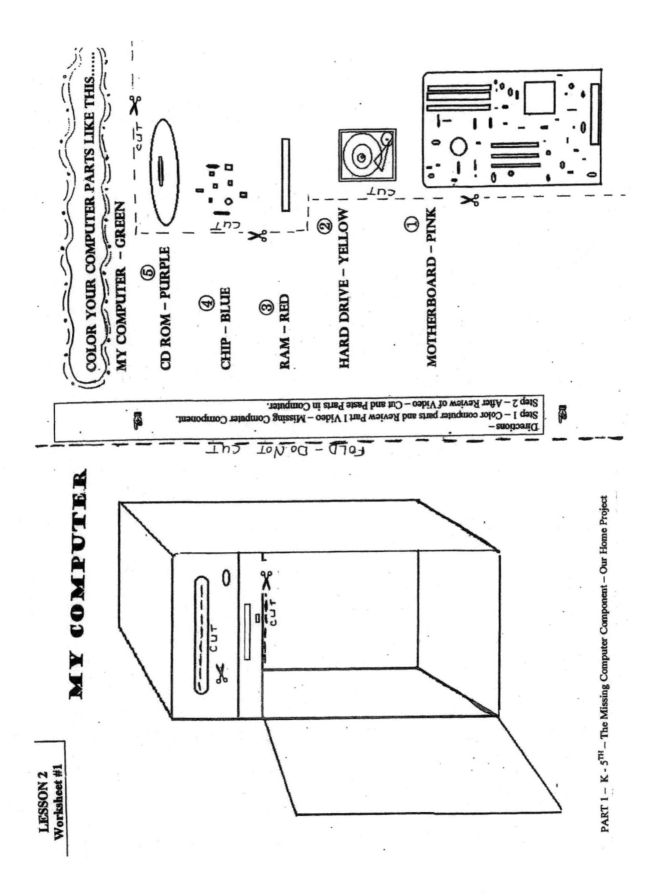

LESSON 2
Worksheet #1

MY COMPUTER

COLOR YOUR COMPUTER PARTS LIKE THIS.......

MY COMPUTER – GREEN

⑤ CD ROM – PURPLE

④ CHIP – BLUE

③ RAM – RED

② HARD DRIVE – YELLOW

① MOTHERBOARD – PINK

Directions–
Step 1 – Color computer parts and Review Part I Video – Missing Computer Component.
Step 2 – After Review of Video – Cut and Paste Parts in Computer.

FOLD – Do Not Cut

PART 1 – K - 5ᵀᴴ – The Missing Computer Component – Our Home Project

15

NAME THAT COMPONENT FLASHCARDS
Level 3-5 Grades

CHIP

COMPUTER PERSONALITY
COMPUTER CHIP – They are tiny bits of electrical currents inside the computer that remembers and processes information.
REMINDER – We never, ever look inside the computer because of the danger of being shocked by the electricity. Even when the computer is turned off and unplugged it holds electricity.

COMPUTER PUPPET PERSONALITY
PUPPET CHIP – He is a ten year old, African American boy who truly wins the heart of everyone with his talents and good manners. He is very loyal, always showing true friendship to his best friend RAM. He believes and trusts Motherboard, who always wants to do the right thing for the puppets. He is an awesome musician and loves to dance to the RAP song TRAIN WITH THE BRAINS.

17

NAME THAT COMPONNENT FLASHCARDS
Level 3-5 Grades

RAM

Who am I?

COMPUTER PERSONALITY

COMPUTER RAM – Random Access Memory – It is memory needed to run the fun games and programs on the computer. Check the amount of RAM in your computer before installing games or programs to make sure you have enough to run them.

COMPUTER PUPPET PERSONALITY

PUPPET RAM – Random Access Memory – He is a nine year old little boy with fire red hair, who has an attitude to match. He does not like to be bossed and makes that known to all. He is smart and knows that he is the big cheese of all the operations in High Tech Land. Sometimes it gets him in trouble. CHIP tries to keep him quiet, but sometimes it doesn't work out. The only one who can make him speechless is RAINBOW PIXEL

Brain Wave – Check your computer and see how much RAM your computer has. Click once with MOUSE on My Computer on your monitor, then move mouse to properties and right click. This will display the resources of your system where you will find RAM.

NAME THAT COMPONENT FLASHCARDS
LEVEL 3-5 Grades

Who am I?

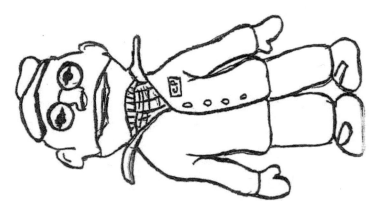

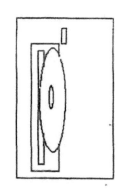

ROM

COMPUTER PERSONALITY
COMPUTER ROM – CD ROM – Read Only
Memory – This is where the fun games are,
put in the computer. Reminder – close all
your games or programs out before taking the
CD out of the CD ROM drawer. If you do not,
you will get the blue error message on your
screen.

COMPUTER PUPPET PERSONALITY
PUPPET ROM – CD ROM – He is the oldest of The
Computer Puppets and loves to ride his dirt bike.
His white hair and pale pink face make him look
like the computer puppet's grandfather, but he
actually just their friend. All the puppets love him
because he is so much fun. Sometimes they forget
how old he is, because he is like so cool!

Brain Wave – To avoid a blue screen error message, always
click on X in upper right hand corner or follow program
directions to close out of program before removing CD from
CD-ROM DRIVE. If you receive the blue screen always try this
first before turning off power switch or rebooting:
☐ PC/Windows – Press Ctrl, Alt, and the Delete Key at the
same time on the KEYBOARD, release and wait for
WINDOWS message window to close program. Then click
on End Task button within window.

21

NAME THAT COMPONENT FLASHCARDS
Level 3-5 Grades

MOTHERBOARD

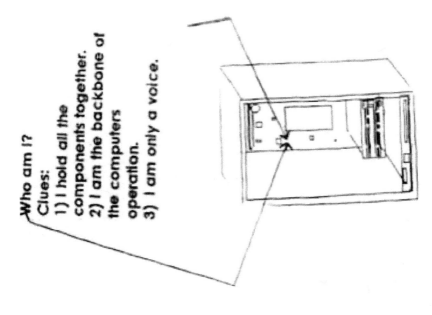

Who am I?
Clues:
1) I hold all the components together.
2) I am the backbone of the computers operation.
3) I am only a voice.

COMPUTER PERSONALITY
COMPUTER MOTHERBOARD – Holds all the components or parts in their proper place inside the computer. A Motherboard is very delicate and must be treated with care. Without Motherboard the computer can not work!

COMPUTER PUPPET PERSONALITY
MOTHERBOARD – Although you never actually see her, you hear her voice of wisdom and know that she always gives protection to all The Computer Puppets. When things get difficult, they always can call on her to give them guidance. She holds High Tech Land together with her touch of understanding and love. If Motherboard is not happy then no one is!

23

IMPORTANT REMINDER TO STUDENTS AND STAFF!
NEVER, NEVER WITHOUT TRAINED TECHNICIAN OR SUPERVISION GO INSIDE
THE COMPUTER OR COMPONENTS HOME!
We never look inside the computer because of the danger of being shocked
by electricity. Even when the computer is not connected to an electrical
outlet the Power Supply inside the computer holds electricity.

Duration

This part is completed over a three–week period. You should integrate it into
your normal computer classroom.

Computer Lab – You may wish to have classroom teacher provide activity of
developing a live program (Lesson 4). The flashcard and discussion – Lesson 5
are suggested within the computer lab.

Objective

- ❑ Provide students with an introduction to how programs are made
- ❑ Introduce the different "languages" that a computer understands
- ❑ Learn how to backup your program or work onto a floppy disk

Learning Outcomes

At the end of this unit, students should:

- ❑ Be familiar with CODE, PROGRAM, ADA, PASCAL & The NOAH BROTHERS
- ❑ Understand the computer language in order to make a program
- ❑ Identify job responsibilities of each Component

Format of Learning Activities

- ❑ Classroom activities – Review Worksheet 6 and follow instructions on
  Lesson 4
- ❑ Video review of Part II
- ❑ Classroom discussion with questions and answers (Flashcards)

Part II

The two twenty-minute classroom activities, detailed below, provide students with an introduction of programming languages and new computer components. They will be introduced to technical terms and given time to interact and enjoy The Computer Puppets. This lesson teaches the importance of PROGRAMMER to the computer and encourages students to think how computer programs are developed.

LESSON 4:   CODE – Classroom Workshop and Discussion

Preparation and Materials

   ✓ Copy of Worksheet #6 – actual code

   ❑ Write out step-by-step directions on how to get to a location within your building
   ❑ Request class to write on the backside of the CODE sheet and tell how they would get to that location from the classroom (If you have an actual layout of school this would work great!)
   ❑ Instructor/Teacher should write directions on the board, making a detailed list as students decide what the instructions should be
   ❑ The MAP of instructions should be detailed with every little item discussed and explained. A way to guide someone to where they need to go by commands and instructions
   ❑ Select a Test Team and a Programming Team to trouble shoot any problems encountered.
   ❑ Select a Student Robot to represent the program and give commands to test the program from list of instructions from class.
   ❑ Explain to class that this is how programs are written. Then request students to attempt to talk to their computer and give verbal commands. Confirm that the computer does not understand English. Just like we don't all understand all verbal languages like Spanish or French, etc.
   ❑ Explain to students that the only person that could tell this computer (robot) how to get to the lunchroom would be a PROGRAMMER (He was in his lab in Part I of The Computer Puppets Show – The Missing Computer Component). The PROGRAMMER understands the computers language and instructs the computer on what to do.

- We called our directions a MAP. What do you think a PROGRAMMER would call his list of instructions? Await response from class. A PROGRAM!
- If we had a very complicated MAP and we had to travel a long distance and a long list of instructions on how to get to where we were going, what kind of things would we need?
    - Transportation
    - Food, water
    - Energy in our bodies to make the trip
- If you were a PROGRAMMER, and you were making your list of instructions in a program. What do you think you would need? You are going to make a really fun program!
    - You would need a computer that would be strong enough to make the trip.
- Which components would you take along on your trip if you were a programmer? Remember this is a fun video game!
    - RAM – because he is the big cheese
    - ROM – because the program would be stored on the CD ROM
    - CHIP – because he helps the computer process the instructions and guides RAM and ROM which way to turn and what to do!
    - The NOAH BROTHERS – because you always need to backup your programs or important data
- Who would be the driver on our journey?
    - Programmer!
- Why?
    - Because he knows the language of the computer and can talk with CHIP, RAM, ROM and all the other Computer Components.
- Could we be the driver in making a program?
    - Yes, if we know the language or the CODE

LESSON 5: VHS Video and Name that Component Flashcards

Preparation and Materials

- ✓ Previous Flashcards from Part I – Worksheets 1–5
- ✓ VHS Video – Part II – Code's Search for More Memory
- ✓ Provide each student with Worksheets 7– CODE, 8 – PROGRAM, 9 – ADA, 10 – PASCAL & 11 – The NOAH BROTHERS
- ✓ Provide crayons for students to color Worksheets 7–11

- Play the VHS – Video – Code's Search for More Memory! Part II – approximately 12 minute video

- After video review the Characters and ask the students why Code needed RAM.

Answer: Because she needed more RAM for the Program that she wanted to become!

- Provide each student with a Worksheets 7 – CODE, 8 – PROGRAM,   9 – ADA, 10 – PASCAL AND 11 – The NOAH BROTHERS
- Review with class each new component that was introduced in video and request they color each as they are being discussed
- Review all flashcards from Part I after coloring is completed. Ask them if they remember what each component's purpose is?

  - RAM – Random Access Memory – He is the Big Cheese. You need him to run the fun games on the computer.

  - ROM – CD ROM is where the fun games are put in the computer. You always close all the programs on your screen by clicking on the X before taking ROM from his home. Blue screen reminder!

  - CHIP – Computer Chips are how the information is stored in the computer. They are electrical currents. REMINDER – We never ever look inside the computer because of the danger of being shocked by electricity. Even when the computer is off, the Power supply inside the computer holds electricity.

  - MOTHERBOARD – She holds all the components. Remind students that she is the backbone of the operation! Make comparisons of their mother to motherboard and how protective a mother is. You can also point out that a Motherboard is very delicate.

NEW COMPONENTS OR PROCESSES

  - CODE – Computer code is machine language that is binary code (010010010) and is how the computer processes the program. An example of this is The Computer Puppets' clothing with 011001101 on them. It takes 8 numbers for 1 alpha character in the computer.

- PROGRAM – A list of instruction given by a programmer to make the computer useful.

- PROGRAMMER – Is a very talented and trained person that understands and can relate to the computer by knowing the language. He is a very logical and a structured individual.

- ADA – Is a general-purpose language and supports real time applications. Has been a mandatory development language for most U.S. Military applications.

- PASCAL – Is a scientific application language used in the development of very complex applications.

- THE NOAH BROTHERS – You should always backup your system to prevent loss of important data files. In the video, you see that it may be the only thing that can save Program. Always be safe and backup your system.

Evaluation

Students should be capable of identifying how different programming languages (HTML, PASCAL and ADA).

- ❑ Journal or verbal reflection on what they learned in each of the activities.
- ❑ Participation in the classroom activities
- ❑ Have the children display their Program (List of Instructions from LESSON 4) in the classroom.

Where to go from here

After confirmation of understanding of how programs are developed proceed with Part III – Somebody Help! Call the Doctor – LESSON 6 & 7. These lessons will reinforce the introduction to components and basic troubleshooting, give an in-depth look at what can happen to a program with a virus, and explain why you need to make backups of your programs.

Worksheet 4 – Html example of Language/Code

```
<html>
<head>
<title>HTML!</title>


</head>
<body background="Homepage!!!!!.jpg"
<img src="../start          " width=82 height=102 alt="Computer Puppets"
border=0 align="left">

<!-- A comment about the code -->

<h1 align="center"><em>HTML!</em></h1>
<p align="center"><font face="Brush Script MT" size="+3"
color="#FF0000">Welcome</font><br>
The <strong>tags</strong> are here somewhere.</p>
<p> </p>
<p> </p>

  .
```

NAME THAT COMPONENT FLASHCARDS
LEVEL 3-5 Grades

CODE

COMPUTER PERSONALITY
COMPUTER CODE- A set of symbols for representing the computers language. It appears as 0's and 1's inside the computer. Code is definitely in control.

COMPUTER PUPPET PERSONALITY
CODE - She is a very determined and bossy ten-year-old girl. Her cute looks and funky blue hair is only a clever disguise for a very controlling individual. She uses Programmer to get her way.

Who am I?

```
<!DOCTYPE HTML PUBLIC "-//w3C//DTD HTML 4.0 Transitional//EN">
<HTML xmlns="http://www.w3.org/TR/REC-html40" xmlns:0=
"urn:schemas-microsoft-com:office" xmlns:'w =
"urn:schemas-microsoft-com:office:word"><HEAD><TITLE><HTML>
-TYPE
<META content=Word.Document name=ProgKb>
<META content="Microsoft Word 9" name=Originator><LINK
```

NAME THAT COMPONENT FLASHCARDS
LEVEL 3-5 Grades

PROGRAM

COMPUTER PERSONALITY

PROGRAM – A set of instructions to tell the computer what to do. You have to follow its directions or the computer will not do what you want it to.

COMPUTER PUPPET PERSONALITY

PROGRAM – She is actually still CODE. She removes her blue hair with the help of PROGRAMMER and becomes PROGRAM, not quite as bossy as CODE but she still is a real control freak. Just don't try to change her without Programmers help. She holds her breath until the screen turns blue. Talk about not acting your age!

Who am I?
Clue: The computer follows my instructions.

35

NAME THAT COMPONENT FLASHCARDS
Level 3-5 Grades

ADA

COMPUTER PERSONALITY
ADA– A high-level programming language developed for use in military systems.

COMPUTER PUPPET PERSONALITY
ADA – She is an eight-year-old Chinese girl with a soft quiet voice, who is a good friend of RAM's. She has one brother named PASCAL. She and PASCAL always travel together. Both are very well known here in the United States for jobs they perform. ADA may be tiny in size, but she carries a lot of power in brains

Who am I?

EXAMPLE OF:

package TABLES is type TABLE is array
(INTEGER range <>) of FLOAT; procedure
BINSEARCH(T: TABLE; SOUGHT:
FLOAT; out LOCATION: INTEGER; out
FOUND: BOOLEAN) is subtype INDEX is
INTEGER range TFIRST..TLAST;

NAME THAT COMPONENT FLASHCARDS
Level 3-5 Grades

PASCAL

COMPUTER PERSONALITY
PASCAL – A high-level programming language. This language is used to write scientific program applications.

COMPUTER PUPPET PERSONALITY
PASCAL – He is an eight-year-old Chinese boy with a very quiet voice and is a good friend of RAM's. He is the brother to ADA and her trusted traveling companion. PASCAL is very gifted in math and uses his gift to solve very complex, scientific problems in our computer world.

Who am I?

EXAMPLE OF:

//PURPOSE: Returns an output string (strOut) that is generated
// from an input string (strIn), by replacing all
// occurrences of one string (strOld) with another
// string (strNew).
//NOTE: No error checking is done so it is up to the caller to

39

NAME THAT COMPONENT FLASHCARDS
Level 3-5 Grades

NOAH BROTHERS

Who are we?

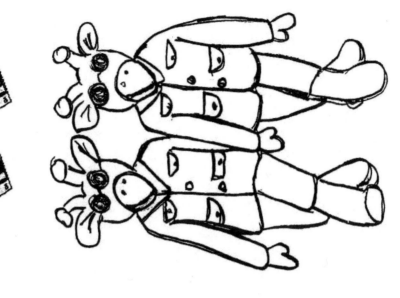

COMPUTER PERSONALITY
THE NOAH BROTHERS – In the computer world, they're backup CD's or disks used in case the original program is broken. All good programmers make sure these are created. You never program without them.

COMPUTER PUPPET PERSONALITY
THE NOAH BROTHERS – They are two very silly giraffes that argue about everything. They are twin Brothers with the same looks, but are very different on the inside. It sometimes hard for Dr. REBOOTY SLY to work with the two of them but he does, because he has no choice! They sometimes hold the only solution to repairs in High Tech Land. They are PROGRAMMER's insurance.

3rd – 5th Grade – Part III – Somebody Help! Call the Doctor!

> **IMPORTANT REMINDER TO STUDENTS AND STAFF!**
> **NEVER, NEVER WITHOUT TRAINED TECHNICIAN OR SUPERVISION GO INSIDE THE COMPUTER OR COMPONENTS HOME!**
> We never look inside the computer because of the danger of being shocked by electricity. Even when the computer is not connected to an electrical outlet the Power Supply inside the computer holds electricity.

Duration

This unit is completed over a three-week period. You should integrate it into your normal computer classroom.

Computer Lab – You may wish to have classroom teacher provide interaction activities. The flashcard and discussion activities are suggested within the computer lab.

Objective

- ❏ Provide students with an understanding of why programs are revised
- ❏ Introduce virus awareness
- ❏ Learn the need for proper back-up of important programs and data

Learning Outcomes

At the end of this unit, students should:

- ❏ Be familiar with program revisions
- ❏ Understand that viruses are not fun and games
- ❏ Know the importance of proper back-up of your system or data
- ❏ Honest PC Awareness

Format of Learning Activities

- ❏ Computer Word Search worksheet 12
- ❏ Video review of Part III – Somebody Help! Call the Doctor!
- ❏ Classroom discussion with questions and answers

The Lesson

The three twenty-minute classroom activities, detailed below, provide students with an introduction of programming languages and new computer components. Students will be introduced to technical terms and given time to interact with and enjoy The Computer Puppets. This lesson will explain the importance of responsible computing.

LESSON 6: RESPONSIBLE COMPUTING WORD SEARCH

Preparation and Materials

- ✓ Copy of Worksheet 12 – Computer Word Search
- ✓ Video – Part III – Somebody Help! Call the Doctor!

- ❑ Provide each student with a copy of Worksheet 12 – Computer Word Search. Complete Computer Word Search while discussing the following:
  - ○ Classroom discussion on "just say no to illegal copies of software". Don't be a Computer Software Pirate.   A Computer pirate is someone that makes copies of software without purchasing them or having a license.
- ❑ Play the VHS Video – Somebody Help! Call the Doctor! – 12 minutes
- ❑ After video, review the characters and ask the students what happened to PROGRAM?

Without the Noah Brothers (The Backups) they could not have restored PROGRAM. They tried to reboot (PRESS CNTRL ALT DELETE on keyboard) PROGRAM but the virus had damaged PROGRAM beyond repair and restoring her with the backups previously made in Part II – Code's Search for More Memory was the only way to save her.

LESSON 7 – Name that Component Flashcards

Materials and Preparations

- ✓ Retrieve Worksheet 1 – My Computer from resource folder.
- ✓ Retrieve all previous Flashcards covered in Parts I & II from resource folder.
- ✓ Provide crayons for new component flashcards

✓ Provide each student with new Flashcards for Worksheets 13 –DR. REBOOTY SLY, 14 – PC TO THE RESCUE, and 15 – BO BYTE, 16 – MEGABYTE, 17 – The Little BITS who are the Mystery components mentioned in Part I – The Missing Computer Component (THE BYTE FAMILY that live on the Hard drive and Floppy Disk)

❑ Provide students with crayons to complete flashcards of newly introduced components.
❑ Request that students identify each component that was discussed in the video
❑ Do they remember what the component does in the computer? Review coloring cut and paste of Worksheet 1 – My Computer and locate the Hard Drive

REVIEW:

○ RAM – Random Access Memory – He is the Big Cheese. You need him to run the fun games on the computer.

○ ROM – CD ROM is where the fun games are put in the computer. You always close all the programs on your screen by clicking on the X before taking ROM from his home. Blue screen reminder!

○ CHIP – Computer Chips are how the information is stored in the computer and it is electrical currents. REMINDER – We never ever look inside the computer because of the danger of being shocked by electricity. Even when the computer is off, the Power supply inside the computer holds electricity.

○ MOTHERBOARD – She holds all the components. Remind students that she is the backbone of the operation! Make comparisons of their mother to motherboard and how protective a mother is. You can also point out that a Motherboard is very delicate.

Part II

○ CODE – She has an attitude and only PROGRAMMER understands her language. This is the language that the computer understands. Binary Code – which is 0110100. Note The Computer Puppets clothes have these numbers on them. It takes 8 digits for one letter of the alphabet.   Programs can be developed in different kinds of languages such as ADA and PASCAL

- ADA – This is a language that the government uses for many government programs.

- PASCAL – This is a programming language that is used for many scientific programs.

- THE NOAH BROTHERS – You should always backup your system to prevent loss of important data files. In the video you see that it is the only thing that saves Program. Always be safe and backup your system.

- PROGRAM – CODE turns into PROGRAM with the help of PROGRAMMER and the use of the RAM memory. A PROGRAM is a list of instructions to tell the computer what to do.

- PROGRAMMER – Is a very talented and trained <u>person</u> that understands and can relate to the computer by knowing the language. He is a very logical and a structured individual.

NEW COMPONENTS OR PROCESSES in "Somebody Help! Call the Doctor!"

- DR. REBOOTY SLY – Stands for rebooting of the system. He is trying to help but sometimes get twisted in thinking and harms the system by expressing himself with error message and bells.

- PC TO THE RESCUE – Is a type of utility software that you would use to hopefully restore your failed system. Examples are Norton and Disk Doctor.

- **THE BYTE FAMILY**

- BO BYTE – A BYTE is composed of 8 consecutive bits. Discuss how the list of instructions that PROGRAMMER gives the computer is stored either on a floppy or hard drive. BO BYTE is introduced as this protective spouse of Megabyte and their seven Little BITS.

- MEGABYTE – A MEGABYTE is used to describe data storage, 1,048,576 (2 TO THE 20th power) bytes. She shows great strength and is carrying a lot of information for everyone. She is very important to the system. She is abbreviated as M or MB.

○ LITTLE BITS – This is the smallest unit of information stored on the computer and is either a 0 or 1. There are seven Little BITS because 8 would make a BYTE.

LESSON 8 – STORING DATA

Materials and Preparations

- ✓ Copy of Worksheet 18 – How Data is Stored
- ✓ 2 Blank Diskettes

- ❏ Review Worksheet 18 as a class
- ❏ Compare the way the diskette is divided into sectors with a subdivision divided into lots.
- ❏ Request that students complete drawing at the bottom of Worksheet 18
- ❏ Instructor/teacher should insert blank FLOPPY DISKETTE in A: drive in the computer
- ❏ Type in the list of instructions to computer – just a brief message to say, "Hello BYTE! This is Mrs. _____ class." Click on Save and watch as the data is stored.
- ❏ Remind students when BYTE has his light on, not to remove the FLOPPY DISK. Wait until he has finished storing the data. Request that they listen to him work as the data is being stored. The Floppy disk is The Byte Family's motor home, and the hard drive is their permanent home.
- ❏ Take a FLOPPY DISKETTE apart and view the inside of it and the actual area where data is stored. CAUTION – Make sure that this diskette does not contain needed information because once it is disassembled it no longer can be put into drive. Please do not try to insert into the DRIVE because it could cause damage to drive.

Evaluation

Students should be capable of identifying the components.

- ❏ Journal or verbal reflection on what they learned in each of the activities.
- ❏ Participation in the classroom activities
- ❏ Have the students display their example of how data is stored on the DISK.

Where to go from here

After confirmation of understanding of how data is stored proceed with Part IV
Activities – Surfing Components! This lesson will give valuable insight to
surfing the web and staying safe.

Worksheet #12 – Computer Word Search

COMPUTER PUPPETS WORD SEARCH

```
P G J M R M T C E H R R N S P
S C A A S Z O L Z Y V S O T R
G R T M E G A B Y T E D A I O
F O G O A Y P O S T R T H B G
H G P E T A W I F R V N B E R
P P U H S H Y W E T R Y R L A
X T I C E U E B U E X E O T M
U O A H I T O R M V L B T T R
A L L T C O T M E R O M H I S
Y D F C T F A E R S L E E L Z
I A A Y Y R O H J E C J R Z C
U S S H G H Z Z I Y H U S E E
L L A O E T Y B O B R P E P D
Y D R A O B R E H T O M O O O
A P J B W E R W O Y A Y X G C
```

ADA
BOBYTE
CHIP
CODE
DRREBOOTYSLY
GOPHERMOUSE
GOPHETTE
LITTLEBITS
MEGABYTE
MOTHERBOARD
NOAHBROTHERS
PASCAL
PCTOTHERESCUE
PROGRAM
PROGRAMMER
RAM
ROM

17 of 17 words were placed into the puzzle.

How data is stored on Disks or Diskette

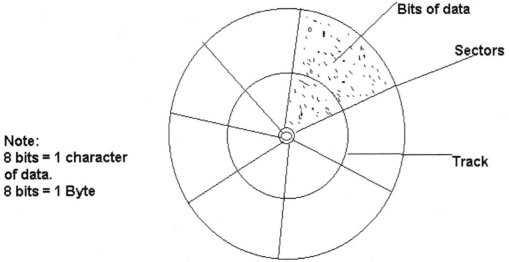

Bits of data

Sectors

Track

Note:
8 bits = 1 character
of data.
8 bits = 1 Byte

Part III - 3-5th - Somebody Help!   Call the Doctor!

Draw an example of disks and how data is stored. Use example as guide.

DR. REBOOTY SLY

COMPUTER PERSONALITY

DR. REBOOTY SLY - This process of rebooting your computer can be handled in several different ways. If you are using a Windows application, you can press Ctrl Alt Del at the same time. This process is used when you are unable to shut the program down by clicking on the X in the upper right-hand corner. Just like the puppet character, this process is a little tricky, and will cause you to loose your information on the screen if you have not saved it.

COMPUTER PUPPET PERSONALITY

DR. REBOOTY SLY - He is a very clever and witty fox with a strange sense of humor. He wants to help people, but at the same time he wants to make them sick. He is a Romeo, who lives the lifestyle of the rich and famous. He loves a challenge and finds it fun to try and outwit BYTE.

Who am I?

Clue: You press Cntrl, Alt and Delete on keyboard and you get me.

NAME THAT COMPONENT FLASHCARDS
Level 3-5 Grades

PC TO THE RESCUE

Who am I?

Clue: I am your 911 Program to recovery.

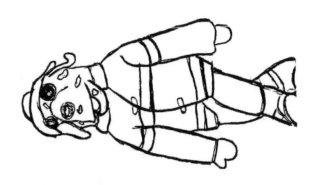

COMPUTER PERSONALITY
PC TO THE RESCUE – Is an example of a repair program used to rescue your hard drive from disaster.

COMPUTER PUPPET PERSONALITY
PC TO THE RESCUE – He is a fireman's emergency Dalmatian dog, with a mission to save the world. He is a super hero who has spent his life trying to rescue all those programs that get harmed by viruses and corruption. He uses his knowledge and tools to save the programs and components. He is a computer's best friend.

NAME THAT COMPONENT FLASHCARDS
Level 3-5 Grades

Who am I?

Clue: I live within the sectors on the floppy or Hard Drive. I am a single character of information.

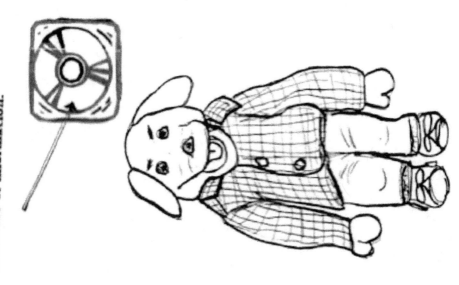

BO BYTE

COMPUTER PERSONALITY
BO BYTE – A group of bits in a row, usually eight, and it represents one unit. A byte is an abbreviation for a binary term, a unit of storage that holds a single character of dat

COMPUTER PUPPET PERSONALITY
BO BYTE – He is a big brown handsome hound dog with a southern accent. He has a deep gruff voice with a personality that is strong but sensitive. He is married to MEGABYTE and will do anything to protect her and his Little BITS from harm. His intelligence is greatly admired by all of The Computer Puppets except Dr. Rebooty SLY, who turns out to be a FOX in Puppet clothes. BYTE is truly a Computer Puppet's best friend.

NAME THAT COMPONENT FLASHCARDS
Level 3-5 Grades

MEGABYTE

COMPUTER PERSONALITY

MEGABYTE – When used to describe data storage, Megabyte is frequently abbreviated as M or MB.

When used to describe data transfer rates, as in MBps, it refers to one million bytes.

COMPUTER PUPPET PERSONALITY

MEGABYTE – She is a beautiful, adorable, curly blonde poodle worth Mega Millions and is always dressed for the occasion. She is an accomplished singer and actress with a heart of gold. Her heart only belongs to BYTE. They met after one of her performances in New York and were soon married. They live in High Tech Land with their adorable seven Little BITS.

Who am I?

Clue: I represent a lot of data storage on the hard drive.

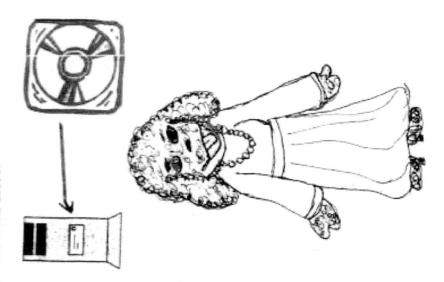

59

NAME THAT COMPONENT FLASHCARDS
Level 3-5 Grades

LITTLE BITS

COMPUTER PERSONALITY

THE LITTLE BITS - A bit is short for binary digit, the smallest unit of information on a machine. A single bit can hold only one of two numbers:
0 or 1.

COMPUTER PUPPET PERSONALITY

THE LITTLE BITS - These seven little BITS are about as adorable as it gets. Imagine seven little brown hound dogs. Four boys and three girls make up this awesome team of fun who always steal the show with their puppy wit and humor. They are the pride and joy of their parents and live in a much protected world of love in High Tech Land.

Who are we?

Clue: If we get one more Little BIT we will be a whole BYTE!

61

3rd – 5th –Part IV – Surfing Components

```
IMPORTANT REMINDER TO STUDENTS AND STAFF!
NEVER, NEVER WITHOUT TRAINED TECHNICIAN OR SUPERVISION GO INSIDE
THE COMPUTER OR COMPONENTS' HOME!
We never look inside the computer because of the danger of being shocked
by electricity. Even when the computer is not connected to an electrical
outlet the Power Supply inside the computer holds electricity.
```

Duration

This unit is completed over a three-week period. You should integrate it into your normal computer classroom.

Computer Lab – You may wish to have classroom teacher provide interaction activities. The flashcard and discussion activities are suggested within the computer lab.

Objectives

- ❑ Provide students with an understanding of how the Internet is set-up. It will give technical terms true meaning
- ❑ Learn to be responsible when surfing the web

Learning Outcomes

At the end of this unit, students should be able to:

- ❑ Safely surf the NET [Internet] with good surfing tips
- ❑ Explain how the Internet is set-up through actual classroom interaction project
- ❑ Identify what is a Computer Crime

Format of Learning Activities

- ❑ Classroom activities – enclosed packet for Part IV – Surfing Components
- ❑ Video review of Part IV
- ❑ Classroom discussion with questions and answers

The Lesson

The three thirty-minute classroom activities, detailed below, provide students with an introduction to the Internet and WEB and demonstrate how to safely surf the Web. They will be introduced to technical terms and given time to interact with and enjoy The Computer Puppets. This part will reinforce the importance of understanding what the Internet and WEB is and how it all works together in making a global connection. This lesson will instruct students on safely surfing the Internet.

LESSON 9 - INTERNET CONSTRUCTION SITE

Materials and Preparation

- ✓ Provide each student with a copy of Worksheet 19
- ✓ 3 x 5 Index cards - 2 per student in classroom
- ✓ Red, Blue and Black Yarn or string
- ✓ Video - Part IV - The Surfing Components

- ❏ Set-up User PC Site - Have students write their name, an email address, and identifying numbers on their Step 1 - Worksheet 19 - Home Computer, as well as, on one of the 3 x 5 index cards. Students should note which service they will be Earthlink (Blue String) or AOL (Red String). Also, have them make up a series of numbers to identify themselves, and then write their number on their index card.
- ❏ Request that students add information about their favorite subject under their identifying number. Punch a hole and attach a long Black string to this index card. This will be their own website and will need to be added to FOLDER 5 in Internet Lesson 9.
- ❏ Review Part IV of Video - The Surfing Components

LESSON 10 - SURFING THE WEB

Materials and Preparation

- ✓ Internet Infrastructure Worksheets 19 - 23 Set-up
- ✓ Website index cards created by class
- ✓ Email addresses and selection of service

Proceed with STEPS Listed below:

STEP 1 – INTERNET ACTIVITY

Request that students add the web pages to the Step 5 Folder – WEBSITE Server. Then put 1 index card with email address and identifying number in this Step 2 folder, ISP Network. Teacher may then make a couple of notes for some of the students to receive, like "Missing Homework!" (Just a suggestion.) Be sure to put their email address on these messages. Suggest you use 3 x 5 index cards to send and receive these messages. Put these in Step 3 Folder.

STEP 2

Select a student to attend STEP 2 Folder – Internet Service Provider Network Folder (ISP). This student will be responsible for deciding if a classmate is a registered user for that service and will forward their connection onto STEP 3 FOLDER. Students should give ID index card with ID number and email address to ISP Student.

STEP 3

Select a student to attend STEP 3 Folder – User Services – This student will be responsible for sorting out email and deciding, which users have mail and sending, at their request, mail back to them. You are then forwarded to the STEP 4 Folder.

STEP 4

Select a student who will decide if the lines will go through AT&T, SPRINT, MCI, Worldcom, QWEST, etc. This ISP Backbone connection with routers/switches will then forward students to the HOST WEBSITES in STEP 5 Folder.

STEP 5

Select a student to be a WEBSITE HOST for Step 5 Activity – This Website Host will be responsible for sorting and finding information when he receives a user's request and will then forward it back across the Internet. Please tell this student that more than one user can request the same subject or site at one time. Request that WEBSITE HOST person add a check mark each time a website if requesting. In the real world this would be accomplished as a counter on the website. At the end of the lesson you can then award the following award ribbons or stickers.

1st Place – Most popular – website with highest search count
2nd Place – Most creative home page (students vote)
3rd Place – Best layout of information (students vote)

STEP 6 – LET'S SURF

After all the above has been accomplished, the remaining students in the classroom will tie appropriate string (Red or Blue) to their Internet Service Provider. They pretend to dial in from their PC Folder and place their string into the STEP 2 Folder to be accepted and authenticated. If the student attending this folder shakes their hand and accepts their string connection then the Step 2 ISP student will forward the line connection to Step 3 User Services student to give them an opportunity to check for mail. Some students may have mail and User Services student will give them this mail. All strings will continue to be forwarded onto Step 4 ISP Backbone. This student at Step 4 will decide which line goes where; such as AT&T, Sprint, and MCI, then forward the line on to STEP 5 Website Host.

In the real world thousands upon thousands of WEB Servers exist and hold all kinds of information. The information is then being carried back across the telephone line or cable connection into your PC. It follows the line connections and number identification given in STEP 4 and STEP 2. This is how it knows to which PC to return this information.

After numerous requests in your classroom for information on this website, you can watch as your classroom becomes the information highway, one GIANT WEB, from requesting and sending of this information to everyone's PC! You may want to rotate students attending Sites to allow all students an opportunity to request information from their PC Card. Ask four students sign off their PCs. Request that students watch what happens to the string as the connections are being returned to their PCs. This will give a meaning to a dropped connection.

DSL – **digital subscriber line** connection. DSL is a very high-speed connection that uses the same wires as a regular telephone line. You are always connected without dialing in. Compare this with cable television.

LESSON 11 – NAME THAT COMPONENT

Materials and Preparation

- ✓ Acquire all Component Flashcards from resource folder

- ❑ Complete final review of component flashcards
- ❑ Request that students identify each component that was discussed in all 4 parts of The Computer Puppet video
- ❑ Do they remember what each of the components or processes do in the computer?

LESSON 12 – I KNOW MY COMPUTER

Materials and Preparation

- ✓ Acquire User PC Site Worksheet #19 from resource folder
- ✓ Worksheet #24 – Input/Output Devices and Computer Parts
- ✓ Scissors and glue for class use

- ❑ Provide each student with a copy of Worksheet #24
- ❑ Classroom discussion about input/output computer devices and computer parts
- ❑ Cut and glue the appropriate labels from devices shown on Worksheet #24 to Worksheet #19 User PC from Student Resource folder

Evaluation

Students should be capable of understanding the basics of the Internet Set-up:

- ❑ Journal or verbal reflection on what they learned in each of the activities.
- ❑ Participation in the classroom activities
- ❑ Have the children display their Website drawing or subject content and information in the classroom or hallway.

Where to go from here

Congratulations you have completed all four parts of our Instructors manual and video production and should have a basic understanding of our technology world. Let's make sure that no component is left unturned. Please continue with The Computer Puppets Board Game. This game will serve as reinforcement for what your students have learned with our Computer Puppets Learning System.

It might be fun to have your students compete with other classrooms or other grade levels in The Computer Puppets Playoffs. This event has been held in past years with great success and gives students the opportunity to share their wealth of knowledge with parents and teachers. It is a goal that students look forward to and work very hard to do their very best in competition. It is fun and educational for both the audience and participants.

INSTRUCTORS RESPONSIBLE COMPUTING Solution

```
R U O Y W I S + + + + + A R D
F + T O + N E + + + + L E A +
+ R N H + F N + + + W V O A +
+ K U + E O D + + A E L T + +
+ + + S + R I + Y N N T + + +
+ + + + M N S + W A + K + +
F S + + A G + O C + E D + +
E L T + + T + D H + E N E + +
M + E R + I Y M + P + O M + +
A A + S A O E L A N O S R E P
I + B + R N + + E + + R O Y +
L + + O T U G + + F + E F L +
+ + + S U + O E + + A P N N +
P A R E N T S Y + + + S I O +
S H A R E + S L I A M E Y O U
```

(Over, Down, Direction)
ABOUT(2,10,SE)
ALWAYS(13,1,SW)
ATTACHMENTS(14,3,SW)
DOWNLOAD(8,8,NE)
EMAIL(1,8,S)
EMAILS(12,15,W)
INFORMATION(6,1,S)
INFORMED(13,14,N)
KEEP(13,6,SW)
KNOW(2,4,NE)
NEVER(10,5,NE)
ONLY(14,14,N)
PARENTS(1,14,E)
PERSON(12,13,N)
PERSONAL(15,10,W)
SAFELY(12,14,NW)
SENDING(7,1,S)
SHARE(1,15,E)
STRANGE(2,7,SE)
SURF(4,5,NW)
THE(3,2,SE)
YOU(13,15,E)
YOUR(4,1,W)
YOURSELF(8,14,NW)

Request that each student write in space provide a good rule from those words
given in the puzzle.
What should you never do?
What should you always do?

Example:
Never share personal information about yourself.
Always keep your parents informed of strange emails.
Surf safely and only download attachments if you know the person sending the
email.

RESPONSIBLE COMPUTING

R	U	O	Y	W	I	S	N	D	P	W	Y	A	R	D
F	Z	T	O	F	N	E	R	J	C	T	L	E	A	X
T	R	N	H	E	F	N	B	L	T	W	V	O	A	N
K	K	U	O	E	O	D	G	Q	A	E	L	T	H	L
F	D	X	S	J	R	I	K	Y	N	N	T	Y	R	W
T	N	B	H	U	M	N	S	T	W	A	P	K	H	O
F	S	U	G	H	A	G	I	O	C	R	E	D	A	Y
E	L	T	K	P	T	A	D	H	W	E	N	E	A	X
M	D	E	R	S	I	Y	M	J	P	Q	O	M	U	K
A	A	P	S	A	O	E	L	A	N	O	S	R	E	P
I	G	B	E	R	N	S	N	E	E	R	R	O	Y	U
L	S	L	O	T	U	G	O	D	F	V	E	F	L	X
Z	Q	F	S	U	I	O	E	D	A	A	P	N	N	S
P	A	R	E	N	T	S	Y	B	S	O	S	I	O	S
S	H	A	R	E	O	S	L	I	A	M	E	Y	O	U

ABOUT	ALWAYS	ATTACHMENTS
DOWNLOAD	EMAIL	EMAILS
INFORMATION	INFORMED	KEEP
KNOW	NEVER	ONLY
PARENTS	PERSON	PERSONAL
SAFELY	SENDING	SHARE
STRANGE	SURF	THE
YOU	YOUR	YOURSELF

24 of 24 words were placed into the puzzle.

Write a good rule to remember using the combination of words above when you surf the Internet.

LOOK AND THINK ABOUT HOW YOU USE EACH PART!

CUT AND PASTE THE FOLLOWING TO THE APPROPRIATE COMPUTER
DEVICES ON WORKSHEET 19– STUDENT PC:

| INPUT DEVICE | INPUT | INPUT |

| OUTPUT | OUTPUT |

| KEYBOARD | MONITOR | MOUSE |

| SPEAKER | CD ROM DRIVE | A: FLOPPY |

| CPU – CENTRAL PROCESSING UNIT |

LESSON 9
Worksheet #19

TEACHER RESOURCE GUIDE

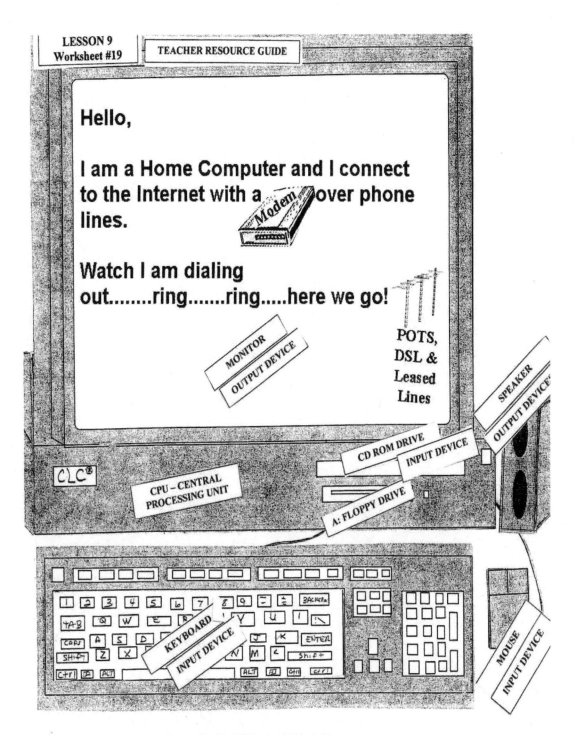

PART IV SURFING COMPONENTS
Step 1 - INTERNET ACTIVITY
STUDENT PC

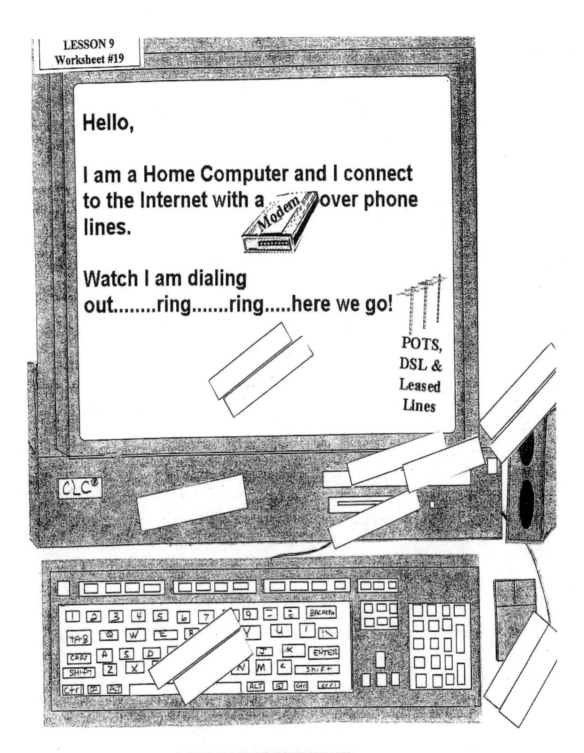

PART IV SURFING COMPONENTS
Step 1 - INTERNET ACTIVITY
STUDENT PC

Hello Again,

You have arrived at the ISP Network. Your connections are being accepted and authenticated here. Good hand shake . . .

User ISP

Looks like they know you! Hold on to your mouse and get ready your on your way to User Services....

CLC®

PART IV SURFING COMPONENTS
Step 2 - INTERNET ACTIVITY
INTERNET SERVICE PROVIDER (ISP)

Welcome to User Services. Hope your travels within the Internet are going well. Oh! I almost forgot we have mail! E-mail

I would really never forget because I am one of the largest and fastest storage servers.

PART IV SURFING COMPONENTS
Step 3 - INTERNET ACTIVITY
USERS SERVICES - EMAIL

Wow! You have arrived at the ISP Backbone. Large Capacity Circuits, Routers/Switches a lot of connections

These are big guys like AT & T, Sprint, MCI, Worldcom, Qwest and the list goes on. We are the Internet connection to the Online content where you get to look at all that stuff!

PART IV SURFING COMPONENTS
Step 4 - INTERNET ACTIVITY
ISP BACKBONE - EX. AT & T, SPRINT, MCI, QWEST

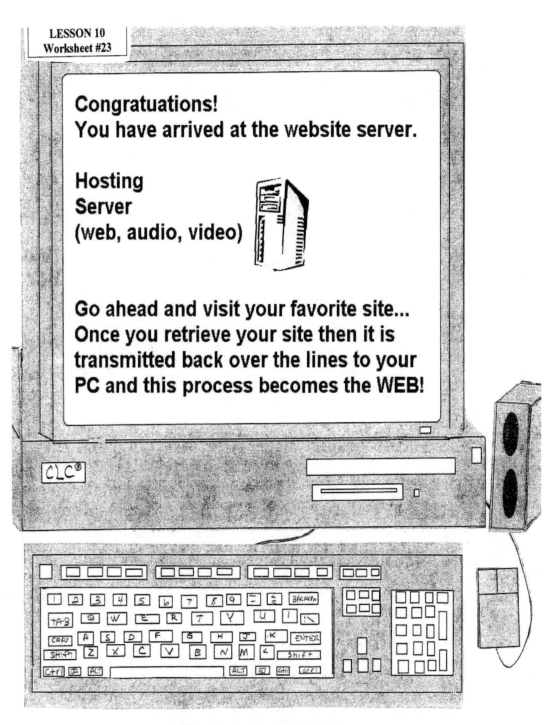

Congratuations!
You have arrived at the website server.

Hosting
Server
(web, audio, video)

Go ahead and visit your favorite site...
Once you retrieve your site then it is
transmitted back over the lines to your
PC and this process becomes the WEB!

CLC®

PART IV SURFING COMPONENTS
Step 5 - INTERNET ACTIVITY
WEBSITE HOST - SERVERS WHERE INFO IS KEPT

Stranger is a Stranger

I'm in the Park.
I'm not alone but my Mommy is on the phone.
A Stranger comes and wants to play.
What will I do?
What will I say?
Where will I go?
So, it's okay.
I yell, "Stranger, Stranger" and I run away.
I find my Mommy and it's okay!

Ten years later, I'm on the NET.
Stranger leaves a real bad text.
He wants to meet me!
So, what's the threat?
What will I do?
What will I say?
He seems so harmless in many ways.
But, he is still hiding in his words.
I hold my breath and then I pray.
I find my parents and it's okay!

So, remember when you're on the NET.
Don't give in to all those threats.
A Stranger is a Stranger in person or on the Internet.

All my best,
MotherBoard

Glossary

Ada

A high-level programming language developed in the late 1970s and early 1980s for the United States Defense Department. Ada was developed to be a general-purpose language for everything from business applications to rocket guidance systems. Ada incorporates modular techniques that make it easier to build and maintain large systems. Since 1986, Ada has been the mandatory development language for most U.S. military applications. In addition, Ada is often the language of choice for large systems that require real-time processing, such as banking and air traffic control systems.

Ada Computer Language is named after Augusta Ada Byron (1815-52), daughter of Lord Byron, and Countess of Lovelace. She helped Charles Babbage develop programs for the analytic engine, the first mechanical computer. She is considered by many to be the world's first programmer.

Application Program

Software designed for a specific purpose (such as accounts receivable, billing, or inventory control). A Programmer is given the needs of the customers and they work with the language selected to accomplish the tasks needed.

Artificial Intelligence, AI

The branch of computer science concerned with making computers behave like humans. The term was coined in 1956 by John McCarthy at the Massachusetts Institute of Technology. Artificial intelligence includes

> ➤ expert systems: programming computers to make decisions in real-life situations (for example, some expert systems help doctors diagnose diseases based on symptoms)
> ➤ natural language: programming computers to understand natural human languages
> ➤ games playing: programming computers to play games such as chess and checkers
> ➤ neutral networks: Systems that simulate intelligence by attempting to reproduce the types of physical connections that occur in animal brains
> ➤ robotics: programming computers to see and hear and react to other sensory stimuli

Currently, no computers exhibit full artificial intelligence (that is, are able to simulate human behavior). The greatest advances have occurred in the field of games playing. The best computer chess programs are now capable of beating humans. In May 1997, an IBM super-computer called Deep Blue defeated world chess champion Gary Kasparov in a chess match.

In the area of robotics, computers are now widely used in assembly plants, but they are capable only of very limited tasks. Robots have great difficulty identifying objects based on appearance or feel, and they still move and handle objects clumsily.

Natural-language processing offers the greatest potential rewards because it would allow people to interact with computers without needing any specialized knowledge. You could simply walk up to a computer and talk to it. Unfortunately, programming computers to understand natural languages has proved to be more difficult than originally thought. Some rudimentary translation systems that translate from one human language to another are in existence, but they are not nearly as good as human translators. There are also voice recognition systems that can convert spoken sounds into written words, but they do not understand what they are writing; they simply take dictation. Even these systems are quite limited -- you must speak slowly and distinctly.

In the early 1980s, expert systems were believed to represent the future of artificial intelligence and of computers in general. To date, however, they have not lived up to expectations. Many expert systems help human experts in such fields as medicine and engineering, but they are very expensive to produce and are helpful only in special situations.

Today, the hottest area of artificial intelligence is neural networks, which are proving successful in a number of disciplines such as voice recognition and natural-language processing.

There are several programming languages that are known as AI languages because they are used almost exclusively for AI applications. The two most common are LISP and PROLOG.

Backup of System

Alternate programs or equipment used in case the original is incapacitated.

BASIC Programming Language

(Beginners All-Purpose Symbolic Instruction Code) A high level interactive programming language frequently used with personal computers. Simple instruction of CODE.

Bit

Short for binary digit, the smallest unit of information on a machine. The term was first used in 1946 by John Tukey, a leading statistician and adviser to five presidents. A single bit can hold only one of two values: 0 or 1. More meaningful information is obtained by combining consecutive bits into larger units. For example, a byte is composed of 8 consecutive bits.

Computers are sometimes classified by the number of bits they can process at one time or by the number of bits they use to represent addresses. These two values are not always the same, which leads to confusion. For example, classifying a computer as a 32-bit machine might mean that its data registers are 32 bits wide or that it uses 32 bits to identify each address in memory. Whereas larger registers make a computer faster, using more bits for addresses enables a machine to support larger programs.

Graphics are also often described by the number of bits used to represent each dot. A 1-bit image is monochrome; an 8-bit image supports 256 colors or grayscales; and a 24- or 32-bit graphic supports true color.

Byte

Abbreviation for binary terms, a unit of storage capable of holding a single character. On almost all modern computers, a byte is equal to 8 bits. Large amounts of memory are indicated in terms of kilobytes (1,024 bytes), megabytes (1,048,576 bytes), and gigabytes (1,073,741,824 bytes). A disk that can hold 1.44 megabytes, for example, is capable of storing approximately 1.4 million characters, or about 3,000 pages of information.

Chip

A small piece of semi conducting material (usually silicon) on which an integrated circuit is embedded. A typical chip is less than ¼-square inches and can contain millions of electronic components (transistors). Computers consist of many chips placed on electronic boards called printed circuit boards.

There are different types of chips. For example, CPU chips (also called microprocessors) contain an entire processing unit, whereas memory chips contain blank memory.

Chips come in a variety of packages. The three most common are:

    ☒ PGAs : Pin-grid arrays are square chips in which the pins are arranged in concentric squares.
    ☒ DIPs : Dual in-line packages are the traditional bug like chips that have anywhere from 8 to 40 legs, evenly divided in two rows.
    ☒ SIPs : Single in-line packages are chips that have just one row of legs in a straight line like a comb.

In addition to these types of chips, there are also single in-line memory modules (SIMMs), which consist of up to nine chips packaged as a single unit.

Code

A set of symbols for representing something. For example, most computers use ASCII codes to represent characters. Written computer instructions. Code can appear in a variety of forms. The code that a programmer writes is called source code. After it has been compiled, it is called object code. Code that is ready to run is called executable code or machine code.

Computer

An electronic symbol manipulating system that's designed and organized to automatically accept and store input data, process them, and produce output results under the direction of a detailed step-by-step stored program of instructions.

Disk

A revolving platter upon which, data and programs are stored.

Hardware

Refers to objects that you can actually touch, like disks, disk drives, monitors, keyboards, printers, boards, and chips. In contrast, software is untouchable. Software exists as ideas, concepts, and symbols, but it has no substance.

Books provide a useful analogy. The pages and the ink are the hardware, while the words, sentences, paragraphs, and the overall meaning are the software. A computer without software is like a book full of blank pages -- you need software to make the computer useful just as you need words to make a book meaningful.

Input Devices

Is the techniques, media, and devices used to achieve human/machine communication. Examples of hardware input devices are; keyboard and mouse.

Internet

Is a massive network of networks, a networking infra structure. It connects millions of computers together globally, forming a network in which any computer can communicate with any other computer as long as they are both connected to the Internet.

Megabyte

When used to describe data storage, 1,048,576 (2 to the 20th power) bytes. Megabyte is frequently abbreviated as M or MB.

When used to describe data transfer rates, as in MBps, it refers to one million bytes.

Motherboard

The main circuit board of a microcomputer. The motherboard contains the connectors for attaching additional boards. Typically, the motherboard contains the CPU, BIOS, memory, mass storage interfaces, serial and parallel ports, expansion slots, and all the controllers required to control standard peripheral devices, such as the display screen, keyboard, and disk drive.

Output Device

Are the techniques, media, and devices used to achieve human/machine communication. Examples of hardware output devices are; monitor, speaker and printer, etc.

Pascal

Is a high level programming language developed by Niklaus Wirth in the late 1960's facilitated the use of the structured programming techniques.

Pixel

The word is short for Picture Element a pixel is a single point in a graphic image. This is the smallest addressable display area on a display screen. Pixels on some displays are square and on others are slightly rectangular.

Program

A set of instructions developed by a Programmer that, when run, causes the computer to perform particular operations: 1) A plan to achieve a problem solution 2) to design, write, and test one or more routines. A list of instructions that the computer can understand.

Programmer

One who designs, writes, tests and maintains computer programs. He understands the language and communicates with the computer through lists of instructions.

Printer

A device used to produce humanly readable computer output. There are a lot of different types of printers such as; dot matrix, ink jets, lasers, etc. with multiple functions. You can fax, copy and scan on some models.

RAM

Acronym for Random Access Memory is a type of computer memory that can be accessed randomly. Ram is the most common type of memory found in computer and other devices, such as printers. Ram is volatile

ROM

Acronym for Read Only Memory on which data has been pre recorded. Once data has been written onto a ROM chip, it cannot be removed and can only be read. Rom is non-volatile.

Software

A set of program, documents, procedures, and routines associated with the operation of a computer system. Contrast with hardware.

World Wide Web

Is a way of accessing information over the medium of the Internet. It is an information-sharing model that is built on top of the Internet. The connection that allows this sharing of information is referred to as the WEB.

Notes

All about Rainbow Pixel of HOPE!

This book is about a beautiful little girl with a heart shaped face and Rainbow colored hair and that lives in a place called High Tech Land. Everyone is depending on her to save them from the dreadful giggly wiggly virus.

The story begins when a little boy name Richie turns his new computer on and Rainbow Pixel appears and asks him for help in saving Motherboard and High Tech Land. He agrees to help and is suddenly drawn into a world that he only thought he understood. The book has several other Computer Puppet characters such as BYTE, MEGABYTE, THE LITTLE BITS, RAM, CHIP and THE WEB.

This story will give a real insight to what a computer virus can do but will show that true friendship and loyally wins over all. This book would help achieve and enhance the following ISTE Standards of 1, 2, 4 & 6.

~~Rainbow Pixel~~

of Hope

by Rene´ Compton

Message to the reader and instructor! I hope you enjoy reading my first technology adventure book with the Computer Puppets. I thought it would be interesting to let you the reader become the illustrator. I have left in all caps what I envisioned for each illustration. It might be fun to have the class share in these illustrations as they go on their technology book adventure with the Computer Puppets!

"Oh, my," RICHIE said, opening the door to see that the deliveryman had a package for him. His new computer had finally arrived, and he could not wait to get it connected. He quickly signed for the delivery and pulled the computer inside the door. The box was smaller than he had expected, but he anxiously opened it.

He connected all the wires and then he plugged it in. He was not prepared for what he heard. Could it be real? How could a computer talk? A single dancing dot appeared on the screen. "What is your name?" the Dot asked.

"Okay, I am sure that this is going to be okay. This is a little strange but hopefully I will get used to this," RICHIE murmured to himself. Then he replied to the Dot, "Hey! Like, I am not supposed to talk to strangers. I feel a little weird telling this to a dot."

"What is this thing that you talk about? Strangers, are they a bad thing? Because, I am not bad," said the tiny dot. "I am a very colorful and talented component and my name is RAINBOW PIXEL." Then suddenly, the computer screen was filled with vivid color.

"Okay! That's cool and you are very colorful I agree, but what exactly are you?" asked RICHIE.

RAINBOW PIXEL quickly replied, "I am a computer component that desperately needs your help."

RICHIE pointed to himself with his eyes wide open in amazement and nervously replied, "What can I possibly do to help you?" Then he added, "Which by the way, I have not agreed to do and you do understand that," said RICHIE in a firm, seeking approval voice.

"Yes," said RAINBOW PIXEL, looking up at him with her big beautiful sequined eyes and nodding her head.

Her beauty was captivating and color surrounded her. "Her rainbow-colored hair seem to flow around her as though she were a mermaid in the sea," thought RICHIE.

And then in a very sweet, innocent voice she replied, "I am in need of human intervention in order to save High-Tech Land. We must find Motherboard. Please, will you help me?"

RICHIE saw how troubled that RAINBOW PIXEL was. Being totally mesmerized by her beauty, he agreed to help.

RAINBOW PIXEL, seeing that she had indeed found someone to help, quickly put her plan into action. She pouted her lips and whispered, "Come closer to the screen." RICHIE was almost face-to-face with RAINBOW PIXEL when she sighed, "Repeat after me. 'See the rainbow follow the stars into computer puppet land afar.' " RICHIE then repeated the words and he suddenly vanished into the screen. He traveled at a very intense rate of speed with RAINBOW PIXEL holding his hand. RICHIE was screeching when everything went black.

The rainbow light reappeared. Inside it were RICHIE and RAINBOW PIXEL. "Where are we?" asked a stunned RICHIE while looking around.

"We are in High-Tech Land," said RAINBOW PIXEL. "Well, what is left of High-Tech Land," she sadly added. Then she indicated, "Hold my hand."

"Oh, no you don't! I am not going on another roller coaster ride with you," exclaimed RICHIE shaking his head.

RAINBOW PIXEL encouraged, "We will not be traveling as fast this time but we must hurry." RICHIE reluctantly took her hand again, and in a rainbow of color they flew through the air looking down over the city streets. RICHIE held on tightly to RAINBOW PIXEL's hand and couldn't help but think how familiar everything looked.

(GIGGLE WIGGLE CITY ILLUSTRATION)

"The city looks very familiar!" yelled RICHIE.

"It should, you use it almost everyday but probably have never seen inside it," explained RAINBOW PIXEL.

"Whoa! This is strange," said RICHIE. "It is like Computer Kingdom." And with that, they suddenly made a sharp turn.

"Oh, no!" fretted RAINBOW PIXEL, "We have to make a detour. Hold on!" They flew at lightning speed through the city and then suddenly vanished into an alley. They finally arrived at what appeared to be the subway. RICHIE, for a brief moment, felt relieved because he thought that they were now in New York City.

He turned to RAINBOW PIXEL and said, "We are in the Big Apple."

"Oh, no!" giggled RAINBOW PIXEL, "We are in a Gateway."

"You mean we are in St. Louis," said RICHIE.

"St. Louis," asked RAINBOW PIXEL looking very confused, "is this some type of new computer you are referring to?"

It was then that RICHIE realized that he was not in a city, but inside a computer. He suddenly felt dizzy, and then he felt faint, and then he fell to the ground. He appeared to be lifeless. RAINBOW PIXEL shook him and tried to wake him up. "Please do not go into sleep mode!" she cried. "This is not a time to rest." RICHIE then opened his eyes, realizing that it was true. He was in High-Tech Land with a rainbow-colored girl! Suddenly RAINBOW PIXEL yelled, "We have got to hide!" And she quickly pulled him inside a folder.

RICHIE, murmuring to himself, "Okay, we are hiding inside a folder in a computer, and I am talking with a rainbow-colored girl. Nobody will ever believe this story!"

RAINBOW PIXEL listened intently to what he said. Flashing her big blue eyes in disappointment at RICHIE, she fumed, "You should never read folders that don't belong to you. You must have seen that this one was labeled personal. It is just not a nice thing to do." RICHIE seeing that RAINBOW PIXEL did not understand what he meant about humans not believing his adventures inside a computer, just nodded his head in agreement with RAINBOW PIXEL.

RAINBOW PIXEL then peaked out of the folder. Turning to RICHIE she whispered, "That was a really close call."

RICHIE, looking very worried, questioned, "A close call. What is wrong?"

"That was the WEB," replied RAINBOW PIXEL, "and if you get caught by her, you will never be the same. Why do you think so many people spend hours and hours just looking at her, RICHIE?"

"Because it is fun!" replied RICHIE.

"Oh, yeah, fun for you humans!" bemoaned RAINBOW PIXEL, "But let me tell you what happens to us components – that is another story. The Web allows people to download viruses. Components and viruses do not get along. I can recall a few of those really bad hair days," she continued. She snubbed her nose with disgust as she thought back to the day her hair was no longer rainbow-colored. "I was suddenly transposed into a green shaky screen of all kinds of weird characters which the WEB referred to as the Slime Crime."

(A PICTURE OF RAINBOW PIXEL WITH A DISGUSTED LOOK ON HER FACE AND ABOVE HER HEAD A THINKING HALLO WITH A PICTURE OF WHAT SHE LOOKED LIKE WITH THE SLIME CRIME.)

RICHIE, seeing that she was getting very upset, quickly added, "By the way, why are we waiting here?"

"We will need to take the subway to BYTE's domain. He will know where to find CHIP and RAM. Hopefully, they can help us find Motherboard," replied RAINBOW PIXEL as she continually scanned each train car with her beautiful blue eyes.

"Which train are you looking for?" asked RICHIE. He also scanned them one by one.

"I would like one, not too fast, but with lots of color and pizzazz," she replied as she shook out her long rainbow-colored hair. "I will know it when I see it," she quickly added.

"But, how do you know that this train will take you to BYTE's domain?" asked RICHIE with a worried look on his face.

(PICTURE OF THEM WATCHING A TRAIN CAR GO BY.)

With the confidence of a true leader, she quickly stated, "Oh! They all lead to BYTE's domain eventually."   She paused and put her very delicate hand to her heart-shaped mouth and replied, "Now, let me see." Meanwhile the cars continued to pass, each one holding a different group of characters.

RICHIE suddenly noticed a car filled with the toy soldier men. He yelled and pointed at the upcoming car. "RAINBOW PIXEL, I think they could help us find Motherboard."

RAINBOW PIXEL quickly replied, "Not a chance! I want color, and they are all very green – bad hair day green," she scrunched her face in disgust. "Anyway they look totally boring and I need fun. Do you hear me? I need fun!" said RAINBOW PIXEL shaking her rainbow-colored head.

"I thought that you needed to find Motherboard and quickly," sighed RICHIE.

"I must clear my mind first in order to remember the directions to BYTE's house," she replied as she tilted her chin up with what appeared to be the confidence of a true soldier. "The best way I know to accomplish this is to take the correct train. Now don't worry, I will know the right train when I see it," added RAINBOW PIXEL with a final nod of her head. Several more train cars traveled by with several more cartoon characters in them. RAINBOW PIXEL shook her head no and looked very disappointed as each car approached. Suddenly she exclaimed, "This is it, RICHIE!" and quickly grabbed him by the hand. They both rushed to jump onto the train.

RICHIE is a little surprised when they boarded the train. Guess who was waiting at the door? None other than two colorful giraffee's named the Noah Brothers, which are good friends of RAINBOW PIXEL's. "They appear to know everything," thought Richie.

RAINBOW PIXEL is delighted to see them and quickly she begins talking and laughing and having a great time with them.

In the meantime, RICHIE was sitting impatiently, waiting on RAINBOW PIXEL for some directions.   Finally, he had waited as long as he could. He turned to RAINBOW PIXEL and anxiously began to question her, "Where are we going, RAINBOW PIXEL?"

"Duh! We are going to save Motherboard," said RAINBOW PIXEL, "but first we have to get some backup."

"We could call the police," said RICHIE.

"The police! What is that?" asked RAINBOW PIXEL.

"You know, the guys that protect the city," he replied.

"Oh! You mean PC Patrol, but they cannot help us now. We must get to Motherboard, and the only way is to get BYTE, RAM and CHIP to help. They will have the answer to finding Motherboard; because, without Motherboard we are all doomed silly," said RAINBOW PIXEL with a fearful expression on her face.

"Okay! I think it might be time for me to go home," said a very concerned RICHIE.

"You can't leave, RICHIE, until we repair all the circuits to get you home. Motherboard is the only way to return you to your world. We don't want to end up like those poor giggling and wiggling components," replied RAINBOW PIXEL. She put her arm around RICHIE as they both gazed out of the train window to a city of very silly acting programs. They were all giggling uncontrollably and wiggling like they had ants in their folders.

RAINBOW PIXEL suddenly jumped to her feet and bid farewell to all the characters. She grasped RICHIE's hand, jumping from the train with one giant leap.

(A PICTURE OF PIXEL AND RICHIE JUMPING FROM TRAIN CAR.)

RICHIE screamed, "Please, slow down!" But RAINBOW PIXEL was only moving faster. They flew through the streets and stopped at C DRIVE. RAINBOW PIXEL, not letting go of RICHIE's hand, rushed to the door. She rang the doorbell and they waited.

BYTE heard the doorbell. He cautiously looked through the peephole and before asking, "RAINBOW PIXEL, who is that with you?" She explained that she had brought her human friend to try to help find Motherboard.

RICHIE, already nervous from hearing BYTE's gruff voice, interrupted, "Hello, my name is RICHIE."

BYTE quickly opened the door and invited them in. RICHIE, staying close to RAINBOW PIXEL, listened as RAINBOW PIXEL explained what had happened in High-Tech Land. She described how almost all the programs were giggling and wiggling with the last downloaded file from the WEB. She ended with, "It is only a matter of time until all the components will be tickled by the WEB to the point of insanity."

BYTE looked very concerned. He then realized that he must send all his BIT's away with MEGABYTE for their safety. He called to his wife, MEGABYTE, and explained to her that the giggling wiggly virus was taking over High-Tech Land. She quickly loaded the floppy disk drive with the Little BIT's and softly kissed BYTE goodbye. She did not want to see seven little BIT's with the giggly wiggles. It would definitely not be good a good thing to experience.

"I will send for you as soon as High-Tech Land is safe again," he choked with tears in his eyes. "Now, my sweet Little BIT's take good care of your mother and we will soon be together again," he continued, trying to reassure them in his strong, protective voice. BYTE then softly kissed each Little BIT goodbye.

Meg looked into BYTE's eyes and softly told him,"don't worry darling, we will be fine. Please be careful. We know you must help save our home and friends in High-Tech Land from this dreadful laughing insanity."

MEGABYTE drove away while The BIT's yelled in unison, "We love you, Pa Pa!"

(A PICTURE OF MEGABYTE AND THE LITTLE BITS WAVING GOODBYE TO BO BYTE FROM THE FLOPPY DRIVE.)

BYTE slowly turned and walked back to his home feeling empty inside. As he opened the door, he realized that RAINBOW PIXEL and RICHIE were waiting for him. They must get down to the business of saving High-Tech Land. He briskly walked with RAINBOW PIXEL and RICHIE closely following behind to the computer room. Turned on the light and sat down at the computer. He then explained to RAINBOW PIXEL and RICHIE, "This message was received from Motherboard days ago. 'I am doing fine and will be in a protected environment until you can bring human intervention to help us recover our city. You must hurry, because we are all weak from continuous giggling and wiggling of bad data from you know who! Signed, you're ever-loving Motherboard. P.S. I will send a message to RAM and CHIP to update my location. I must keep moving because the wiggles are worse than the giggles.' "

"BYTE, do you know where RAM and CHIP live?" asked RAINBOW PIXEL.

BYTE replied, "Of course on normal days we see each other regularly but this has not been a normal day. I have not seen them since yesterday."

"Oh! I hope the dreaded WEB has not," RAINBOW PIXEL paused and said, "done something dreadful to them." RAINBOW PIXEL began to cry knowing that RAM and CHIP could be their only hope in saving High-Tech Land and now they possibly could be giggling and wiggling out of control.

RICHIE was a little surprised to see RAINBOW PIXEL cry; she had seemed so confidant. And after-all, she was a component. RICHIE held her and reassured her that it would be okay. They would find them. "Oh well," he thought, "this is a little weird but this entire day has been really weird."

They all got in the Bytemobile and flew far from the city when suddenly the radar beeped. "Looks like the radar is picking up something or someone in that field. Maybe it is RAM and CHIP," said BYTE.

They swirled through the sky and landed in a big field of clover. When they got out of the Bytemobile, RAINBOW PIXEL displayed her rainbow of color to alert RAM and CHIP of her arrival in case they were actually there. Soon out of the field emerged RAM and CHIP. They were not what RICHIE had expected but nothing had appeared normal today. RAM was very handsome and carried himself with dignity but worry was reflected in his face. CHIP was awesome – just a totally cool dude with what appeared to be a passion for excitement.

RAINBOW PIXEL had never before met RAM face-to-face. Both seemed pleased to meet one another. CHIP was busy talking with BYTE about how to find MotherBoard. Bang! Sizzle! Sparks were flying! RAM held RAINBOW PIXEL close to protect her from the falling wiggling giggling program. Soon the giggling stopped but it was still wiggling out of control. It finally disappeared from site. RAM reluctantly let go of RAINBOW PIXEL's hand.

RAM then stood up and said, "Motherboard has contacted us. She gave us a riddle, but according to her instructions only a Human can decode it."

CHIP unfolded the piece of paper with the instructions and handed it to RICHIE. RICHIE was totally confused by what he read on the paper. He read it again and again out loud, "'You must go through the loop and then the hoop but beware of the doggy poop. You must not be unkind. Then you must gather your finds and get in a line to see the magic show. You will see inside the little tree to me.' Oh, boy! Are you sure I am the guy for the job?"

RAINBOW PIXEL sadly replied, "You have to be; without you we will all giggle and wiggle forever."

Trying to encourage RICHIE, CHIP said,"I know you can do it. It's just a little riddle. After all, you humans love riddles. Don't you?"

RICHIE responded, "We normally are not solving riddles to stop programs from the giggle wiggle. Why can't she just tell us where she is?"

RAM then told RICHIE, "Motherboard knows that at any time a component could be captured. And without the capability of solving riddles, we are safe from being interrogated. She is only trying to protect us from the giggle wiggle virus. We could possibly be the only sane components left in High Tech Land."

"We will be under close surveillance in High-Tech Land and giggle wiggles will be all around us. Remember we need your human intervention to help us solve the riddle," added CHIP.

RAINBOW PIXEL looked at RICHIE and said, "Please, RICHIE, I know you can solve the riddle, if you try."

RICHIE instructed everyone, "Get in the BYTEMOBILE, and I will do my best to try and find Motherboard."

They flew across the sky once again with RICHIE looking at the riddle, repeating it over and over. "Okay! Let me think about this. 'You go through the loop and then the hoop.' " RICHIE suddenly yelled out, "Turn here! It means a loop where we do the same thing over and over." The Bytemobile turned onto the highway and looped and looped. They were on what appeared to be a giant roller coaster. They were all screaming and holding on for dear life. It was as though it would never stop looping.

(A PICTURE OF THEM LOOPING IN THE BYTEMOBILE.)

Dizzily BYTE yelled, "Now what, RICHIE?"

RICHIE yelled back just as loudly, "Find the hoop off the loop." Everyone frantically searched for a hoop as they whirled around.

Then suddenly BYTE viewed the hoop. Without warning, he turned the Bytemobile onto the off ramp shouting, "Here it is!" The Bytemobile jumped through the hoop. Coming to an abrupt stop, BYTE hopped from the Bytemobile and started running without waiting for the others.

"Where is he going?" asked RICHIE.

CHIP, seeing where BYTE was running, started to laugh and replied, "I believe that doggy has got to poop." The car filled with laughter.

RICHIE suddenly realized it was all part of the riddle. He attempted to calm the laughing components by shouting, "Be quiet! Remember the next part of the riddle. 'You must not be unkind. Then you must gather your finds and get in a line to see the magic show. You will see inside the little tree to me. As hard as it was, they all tried to hold back their laughter as BYTE returned to the Bytemobile.

Pulling away from the curb, the Bytemobile was soon spinning in the air. They had flown a very short distance when suddenly in front of them they saw a tree.

"Oh boy, now that's a tree!" exclaimed CHIP.

(A PICTURE OF A BIG TREE AND ALL OF THEM PEERING INSIDE)

"Should we go inside?" questioned BYTE.

"No wait! The Riddle said we must gather our finds and get in a line to see a magic show," said RAINBOW PIXEL.

RAM then looked into RAINBOW PIXEL's big blue eyes and sighed, "I have my find, the love of my life." RAINBOW PIXEL glowed like a rainbow with RAM's words. When she touched the bark, the tree opened up like magic.

RICHIE screamed, "Everyone gets into a line so we can find Motherboard." They all hurriedly got into a line and disappeared into the tree. Not knowing what to expect, they soon were falling down a long, narrow tunnel that never seemed to end. At last the tunnel ended with all of them tumbling to an abrupt stop in front of a huge red door.

"Now what do we do?" asked RICHIE.

"We should find Motherboard," said RAINBOW PIXEL.

"No one has actually ever seen Motherboard," explained RAM, "but we know she is there."

"I am sure we should just wait for directions," said CHIP. He pulled out a deck of cards and asked, "Does anybody want to play?"

"Really!" said RAM in a very annoyed tone of voice, "At a time like this, you want to play cards?"

"Sure," replied CHIP, "not much else we can do until we are contacted by Motherboard."

It was at that moment that the red door opened and a bright light appeared. A voice spoke from the light, "Hello, my components and human friend. Welcome to my home. Please come in and have some <u>cookies</u>."

"Wait!" cried RAM. "Something is not right. It is just a feeling I have deep in my component.

RICHIE, thinking out loud, replied, "Now that's weird. I would have said I have a feeling in my gut."

A puzzled RAINBOW PIXEL asked, "Your gut. What is that, RICHIE?"

"Oh! Don't worry, but let's not rush into a bad situation. We should repeat the riddle to make sure we have followed all the directions accordingly," encouraged RICHIE. He began to read the riddle out loud one more time. "'You must go through the loop and then the hoop but beware of the doggy poop. You must not be unkind. Then you must gather your finds and get in a line to see the magic show. You will see inside the little tree to me.'"

"Oh no! It's a trap, we are in the wrong tree," yelled RICHIE. They all frantically tried to crawl back up the tunnel; however, when they tried to leave the Web wrapped around them. BYTE chewed it away as quickly as he could with RICHIE following close behind him. RAINBOW PIXEL was so delicate that the Web had surrounded her, and she could not escape.

Looking back over his shoulder, CHIP warned, "Oh no! RAINBOW PIXEL is in trouble. The WEB is making her into a Dot of cotton candy!"

After hearing this, RAM returned to help. He began to sing "She Is Not Just a Dot.

She means much more to me. She's all I've got.
I just can't leave her now. Don't you see?
She would help, if it were me!
Whooooooah!

She's not just a Dot.
Our love will save us and it's all we've got.
We'll join together and we'll soon be free.
My Little RAINBOW PIXEL don't let go of me.

Whooooah!
She's not just a Dot!"

When his hand finally reached her hand, it warmed her heart, and soon the Web began to melt from her. He pulled her from the Web, and they climbed as fast as they could to the top of the tunnel.

(A PICTURE OF RAM SINGING TO A RAINBOW PIXEL ALL COVERED WITH A WEB.)

When they had all reached the daylight, they realized that there had actually been two trees, a big one and a little one. Now the little tree was lying limp upon the ground. Not knowing what to do, they all sat down in desperation.

RICHIE moaned, "We can't give up. We still must find Motherboard. She probably had to leave because the WEB showed up. We need to search for clues." They all looked at RICHIE confused about looking for clues. He realized they did not understand everything in his language, so he explained, "We need to look for more directions." They all nodded their heads in agreement and began to scan the surrounding grounds.

They were about to give up when a small flicker of light flashed across the sky. RAM instantly stood up and excitedly explained, "Motherboard is sending us another message."

RICHIE looked at them and said, "Don't look at me! I am just the Riddle Man."

RAM laughed, "Don't worry, RICHIE. CHIP and I can decode this one." They watched and recorded what Motherboard was sending to them. A very relieved RICHIE patiently waited.

RAINBOW PIXEL with a worried look on her face asked RAM, "Is Motherboard okay?"

"Yes!" RAM replied sadly. "She is okay, but is concerned for all of High-Tech Land. She said that we only have two hours to rescue her. After that it will be too late."

RAM turned to RICHIE, "What time is it?"

"It is 2:15 pm," replied RICHIE.

"Thank you!" said RAM. "According to Motherboard, the WEB has almost completely taken over High-Tech Land. RICHIE you are our only hope. If we can get you to Motherboard, then hopefully you can repair the damaged circuit."

(A PICTURE OF RICHIE LOOKING AT HIS WATCH WITH A WORRIED LOOK ON HIS FACE.)

RICHIE said, "I will be happy to do what I can, but if we can't find Motherboard, then how am I going to repair the circuit?"

CHIP agreed, "The guy is right you know!" They all did realize that without finding Motherboard it was hopeless. But they would not give up.

"Look again at what Motherboard's message said. Maybe you missed something," prodded BYTE. RAM and CHIP reviewed the message and confirmed that they did not see anything. BYTE insisted that RICHIE review the message, also. RICHIE picked up the message and slowly began to read it.

"If Motherboard is trying to send us a message then it must be in code," explained RICHIE. "'High-Tech Land' and 'two hours' does this mean anything?"

RAINBOW PIXEL thought aloud, "I once watched a performance at the Two Hour Club in High-Tech Land. How would Motherboard have known that?"

"Remember that Motherboard is always there, but you just don't know it," said RAM. "What was the performance that you saw? Maybe you saw something that could help us."

RAINBOW PIXEL paused, "It was called, 'The Best Days of Summer'. I just don't understand how that could possibly have some meaning to where she is."

"What did the stage look like?" asked CHIP. "There must be some meaning to all of this. But what?"

At that moment the light flashed again, but this time it was short. RAM and CHIP recorded this latest message. "Motherboard said to enjoy the tea cakes," said a puzzled RAM.

Then suddenly it was clear to RAINBOW PIXEL. She remembered that after 'The Best Days of Summer' performance, she had gone to a little restaurant in China Town called he Best of the Twollies, which was infamous for their tea cakes. Excitingly she exclaimed, "I know where Motherboard wants us to go. Follow me to China Town."

They all cheered in agreement, "What are we waiting for?"

"Let's get going," said CHIP. They all climbed into the Bytemobile. RAM programmed the Bytemobile to the exact location, and they took off for China Town. They arrived in record time.

(A PICTURE OF ALL OF THEM IN THE BYTEMOBILE IN CHINA TOWN)

From the information that RAINBOW PIXEL had given, they had a plan by the time they arrived. RICHIE strolled into the restaurant alone to check it out. He ordered the tea cakes as RAINBOW PIXEL had suggested. Inside the tea cake was another message, so he hurriedly paid the bill, raced outside to the Bytemobile, and gave the message to the others.

RAM read as he instructed BYTE to drive to 100 PC Drive. However, as they were about to pull away from the curb, they heard giggling and wiggling components. They covered the streets and the air was filled with uncontrollable giggles. "There is no runway for the Bytemobile to take off," exclaimed BYTE. "We will have to try to make it on foot, or we will run out of time." They all got out of Bytemobile and ran towards 100 PC Drive except for Little RAINBOW PIXEL. She grabbed RAM's hand and flew through the sky.

(A PICTURE OF RAINBOW PIXEL AND RAM FLYING THROUGH THE AIR)

RAINBOW PIXEL and RAM arrived first with the others close behind. They hurried up to the door and rang the doorbell. At last they had found Motherboard and she could no longer control her giggles and wiggles. RAM and CHIP assured everyone that it was going to be okay. RAINBOW PIXEL turned to RICHIE, "What time do you have?"

"It is 4:00 pm, which means we only have 15 minutes to save Motherboard and High-Tech Land," replied RICHIE. "We have to work fast." RICHIE began trying to connect the wires that were frayed from Motherboard, but soon realized that it was not going to work. "We need some type of new connection – something that can generate enough energy to recharge all the components in High-Tech Land," RICHIE explained. "Quickly, BYTE! Go to the BYTEMOBILE and bring me your battery and cables."

BYTE sadly stated, "It is blocks away, and I will never make it by 4:15. We need energy and now!"

"I can help," said RAINBOW PIXEL.

"No!" said RAM, "It could mean your sanity. I can't let you do it RAINBOW PIXEL."

"But, if I don't try RAM," asserted RAINBOW PIXEL, "we will surely giggle and wiggle until we all fall down. I am responsible for bringing RICHIE from his world to help; and I am responsible for seeing him safely home. I have no choice. I must!"

(A PICTURE OF RAINBOW PIXEL TALKING WITH RAM.)

RAM eyes were filled with sadness as RAINBOW PIXEL, with her long rainbow-colored hair gleaming as bright as the stars, reached out her hand to Motherboard. Motherboard was almost lifeless from all the giggling and wiggling, but as the energy was bridged with RAINBOW PIXEL's hair she began to calm the wiggles. RAINBOW PIXEL was getting very weak, however she continued to bridge the connection. The entire land returned to normal, but not little RAINBOW PIXEL.

RAM sat by her side in hopes that she would survive the insanity of the giggles and wiggles.

As she lay lifeless with her hair dulled, not gleaming so brightly, RAM noticed a golden hairpin in her hair. He hurriedly removed it from her hair and handed it to RICHIE. "This is wonderful," said RICHIE. "We can repair Motherboard permanently and hopefully save RAINBOW PIXEL from her awful fate." He frantically began to work, using the hairpin to make the connections. Soon Motherboard was up and running but RAINBOW PIXEL was slowly fading.

(PICTURE OF RAINBOW PIXEL AND RAM SITTING BY HER SIDE HOLDING HER HAND.)

RAM sat holding RAINBOW PIXEL's tiny little hand. He began to sing, "She Is Not Just a Dot.

She means much more to me. She's all I've got.
I just can't leave her now. Don't you see?
She would help, if it were me!

Whoooooah!

She's not just a Dot.
Our love will save us and it's all we've got.
We'll join together and we'll soon be free.
My Little RAINBOW PIXEL don't let go of me.
Whooooah!
She's not just a Dot!"

He watched as the rainbow color refilled her hair. RAINBOW PIXEL slowly opened her glittery blue eyes and smiled at RAM. As soon as she was able to speak without a giggle in her voice, she told RAM that RICHIE must be returned to his home since their land was now free from the giggle wiggles.

RAINBOW PIXEL looked at RICHIE and said, "Thank you for helping to save our land and for saving me from a life of insanity from the giggle wiggle virus."

"Oh! It was not me that saved you, but RAM who found the golden hairpin in your hair," said RICHIE. RAINBOW PIXEL then flashed her adoring smile at RAM, who gleamed with pride.

RAINBOW PIXEL said, "Come closer, RICHIE, and repeat after me. 'See the Rainbow. Follow the stars into your world afar.' "RICHIE repeated it with sadness in his voice. He then disappeared from High–Tech Land and reappeared in the land that he called home.

The End

All about The Computer Pirate!

This book has our favorite two characters CHIP and RAM. They think they are on a nice relaxing vacation of course via a laptop, when suddenly CAM, which is another Computer Puppet character spots some suspicious behavior. Yes, it is a Software Pirate with an entire ship of illegal software copies. This Pirate has captured poor CD ROM and is making him reproduce illegal copies of software. CHIP and RAM devise a plan to save CD and to put this pirate out of business. The two of them analyze the data and decide that a Pirates most treasured possession is a treasure map. They try to capture the treasure map in an effort to prove to the Pirate that it is wrong to take things that do not belong to you. This is pretty risky business for CHIP and RAM but the two of them understand they have to standup for what is right. Programs are just as important to a Programmer as a Pirates treasure map is to him. Hopefully they can help this Pirate understand that.

This story will show how true dedication by just a few can make a big difference in doing the right thing. This book would help achieve and enhance the ISTE Standards of 1,2,3,4 & 5.

The Computer Pirate

By Rene' Compton

Once upon a time there lived a pirate on the Atlantic Ocean who was not

an ordinary pirate, but a Computer Pirate. He stole software from the intellectual brains of the world to sell to those individuals called humans. This pirate was not so nice, and unfortunately, Chip and Ram were about to cross his path.

Programmer had brought Chip and Ram to the Caribbean for a short vacation. This particular day was sunny with Chip and Ram relaxing in the shade of a flowering palm tree. While a gentle breeze blew across them, ever watchful Cam and Molly Monitor, observed everything happening on the island and out over the ocean. As Cam scanned with his one big eye, he noticed a very disturbing site. A pirate's ship had appeared on the horizon. Cam knew that this pirate and his first mate were up to no good. He alerted Chip and Ram that something bad was going to happen with these two evil pirates lurking around.

"Hey! Chip, Ram looks like we have company," reported Cam. "I spy a pirate ship. It looks like it is not an ordinary pirate on board, but Computer Pirate, and he is coming this way."

Ram, looking concerned, quickly turned to Cam and started asking questions, "Who is Computer Pirate, Cam?" Without waiting for a reply, he continued, "Why is he coming to this island?" [Ram had met a few computer villains in his days, but never a pirate!]

Chip quickly saw that Ram was getting himself all upset over this pirate. He knew that Ram probably did not understand that a Computer Pirate was more of a threat to humans than to computer components. Quickly, Chip recommended that Ram should not worry. He suggested that they simply observe the pirate to see what he was up to! At this time, Chip did not realize what kind of danger they would soon encounter.

"Oh, no!" exclaimed Chip. "It is worse than I thought. He is definitely a Computer Pirate! He has the entire ship loaded with illegal copies of software, and he is still making more copies. He is probably going to come on shore to bury the stolen property."

Chip rapidly turned back to Cam to closely observe the pirates' activities on board as the ship sailed closer and closer to the shore. Eventually, he got around to telling Ram about computer pirates. "They are people who make illegal copies of software," he explained. "A lot people use these copies and do not think twice about them being illegal." Chip continued, explaining about many people accepting illegal copies as being okay. However, he made sure Ram understood that a lot of time and money had been invested in making software and that developers were hurt financially because of this type of behavior.

They could still see the pirate making copies aboard the ship and heard his appalling laughter. "Sometimes when you make things too easy for humans, they forget their morals," emphasized Chip. "You know not to take things that don't belong to you.   Well, pirates sort of justify their actions by saying that everyone else is doing it. However, two wrongs don't make a right. Someone has to stand up for what is right!"

Chip rambled on and on until finally Ram said, "Chip, I understand that it is not right, but what can we do about it? " Ram was nervous. He thought maybe they should just turn their heads and pretend that they did not see the pirates' evil deeds. He was tempted, but soon remembered that they had responsibilities.

"Well," Chip reflected, "let's contact Motherboard. She always advises us wisely.   We don't want to act too hastily and end up as fragmented components. After all, we have never encountered a real live Computer Pirate before!"

Reporting to Motherboard, Chip blurted loudly, "Program has been kidnapped by a Computer Pirate, and we need your help!"

"Oh, dear! This is dreadful, Chip!" responded Motherboard.

After listening intently to Motherboard reiterate everything that Chip had stated about computer pirates, Ram was convinced to do the right thing. He now understood that this guy was a serious threat to Programmer and Program. The pirate could be making thousands of copies of Program and selling them without Programmer's consent. Programmer had spent years developing his software programs, not to mention all the money he had invested.

Gaining confidence in his conviction, Ram declared, "Our friend, Program, has been kidnapped by Computer Pirate, and we need to help her. Programmer is our friend, too. This vacation was his idea, so we must do our best to protect both of them."

"Is this pirate by himself on the ship or does he have others helping him?" Motherboard asked.

"From what we have observed, it appears that he has one other person on board. Hurry, Cam, can you get a good look at the other person?" Chip requested. Suddenly their worst nightmare appeared on Molly Monitor. Oh, no! Could it be true?

"How can it be Hacky? After all, we got rid of him months ago. He probably created the worse virus I have ever encountered and I was so relieved when he decided to leave High Tech Land," reflected Chip.

"Maybe he was never really gone, but just hiding in High Tech Land," said RAM. "And, just waiting to show his ugly face. BOO!" yelled Ram.

All the components jumped with fear upon hearing Hacky's name once more. Well, poor Molly Monitor could not even focus, because she was so shaken from fear. Ram and Chip thought it was funny, but Motherboard did not.

She understood how serious the situation was with Hacky present. "Boys, this is serious and you guys need to be more understanding of your friends' feelings," scolded Motherboard.

"We are sorry, Cam and Molly, that we scared you," said Ram and Chip in unison.

"Now, that is better boys," said Motherboard. She continued, "We must show Computer Pirate what it feels like to have something taken from him. Maybe the pirate will understand if he can relate to what others are feeling."

Looking very confused, Ram listened but did not truly understand what they were to do. Motherboard continued, "Watch until Computer Pirate has hidden the pirated software, and then we can make an exact duplicate of his treasure map to steal his treasure."

Chip knew exactly what to do. Putting the plan into action, he soon informed Cam and Ram what each of them needed to do. "This is going to take a lot of close supervision, and we must not be seen by anyone," Chip quietly informed them. "We have to get a clever disguise in order to monitor Computer Pirate's every move while he finds a hiding place for his treasure. For the plan to work, we must make a map that looks exactly like his treasure map."

"But how can we disguise ourselves?" Ram asked.

Chip and Cam thought and thought; nonetheless, they soon knew exactly how they would disguise themselves. Cam had decided that he and Molly would monitor from atop a coconut high up in a tree. They would report back to Chip, who would be busy analyzing the data to make an accurate copy of the pirate's treasure map.

"Ram, you are the adventurous one," said Chip. "Your job is to find a monkey who will be the messenger. I will write a message to Computer Pirate letting him know that we have made a copy of his treasure map, and that we know where his treasure is hidden. The messenger monkey can drop the message from a tree into the pirate's path."

Thinking about the plan, Ram – with his big blue eyes wide with excitement – responded, "This just might work, and we might get this pirate to change his ways. Or, at least feel badly about his actions."

As Cam watched, the pirates loaded their dinghy with the pirated software. Soon they climbed in and began rowing, inching closer to the shoreline. Cam spoke, "They are about to come ashore. Boys, let's get started."

"Everyone get into position," yelled Chip.

Soon they were precisely monitoring and recording the data as Computer Pirate and Hacky moved quietly inland, dug a hole, and buried the containers filled with the illegal software copies. Cam quickly reported back to Chip with the location. Chip busily made the map of how to find the treasure. However, Ram was not having an easy time convincing a monkey to deliver the map.

"Now listen, I will make this worth your while," bribed Ram. "If you successfully drop this treasure map where Computer Pirate can see it, I will convince Programmer to make a fun video game about you. You know, like Monkey Express or Monkey Mail. What do you think?" asked Ram. "Will you do it?"

This monkey just did not appear to be interested in being the star of his own video game. Ram suddenly thought that maybe these little things called 'responsibility' and 'guilt' just might work on animals, too! Well, what did he have to lose at this point? He decided to try a different approach using Motherboard's analogy to something the monkey could relate.

"Listen, monkey. Just suppose this pirate came to your island and stole all the coconuts and bananas that belong to you. Then he tried to steal the trees that grow the coconuts and bananas. Would you sit back and let it happen?" Ram quizzed.

At last, the monkey reached out his hand, took the treasure map, and swung high up into a tree. Ram, looking very relieved, said aloud, "This little thing called responsibility is powerful to both humans and animals!"

Cam and Molly continued to monitor while the monkey swung from tree to tree. Soon he was hanging directly over the pirates. Computer Pirate and Hacky had just finished covering the treasure and were laughing out loud when the monkey did his thing. It was as though the monkey and map were in slow motion. With Cam's help, Motherboard, Ram and Chip all observed the monkey dropping the duplicate map down in front of the pirates. Computer Pirate drew his sword with haste and yelled, "Who goes there?" He picked up the map, glanced at it, and then appeared to become very upset. He inspected the area to see if anyone was there. Upon seeing no one, he paid closer attention to the map. He saw what Chip had written on the bottom.

Dear Mr. Computer Pirate,

We understand that you probably don't care that you steal things, because that is what a pirate does. However, we want you to feel what others feel when you take from them. As you can see, we know where your treasure is buried; but, you don't know where we are. And, we plan to destroy the copies of the illegal programs once you leave the island. Programmer is our friend. We are trying to protect him.

How does it feel to know that your treasure will be stolen, and that there is nothing you can do about it, because you don't know who we are or where we are?

Computer Pirate stood still, but then got angrier, and finally began hitting the tree in front of him with his fists. Bananas fell from the tree. The monkey who had delivered the message was stealthily watching from the treetop while holding on tightly. He had already informed all the other monkeys of what Ram had told him about getting his bananas stolen, and then the coconuts, and then the trees.

As the story was told, from one monkey to the next until all the thousands of monkeys were informed, it had gotten a little mixed up. Before long, the story was that Computer Pirate was there to steal everything from the monkeys. Of course, when they saw the pirate hitting the tree, they thought it was to steal their bananas. The monkeys began to swing above the pirates' heads, dropping coconuts and bananas on top of them.

Chip and Cam could not understand what was happening. Ram watched in amazement as these monkeys were all over this pirate and his friend. Before long, Computer Pirate was begging for someone to get the monkeys off them. Chip and Cam thought the monkeys had gone mad and were frightened to get near. But, ever-adventurous Ram was laughing so hard that he could barely speak. He finally was able to relate the analogy that he had told the monkey when he asked him to deliver the treasure map to the pirates. "I was trying to get the monkey to relate to how it felt to be stolen from, but he must have thought Computer Pirate and Hacky were here to steal everything from the monkeys!" said Ram.

Once Chip understood, he told Ram that he needed to tell the monkeys to leave the pirates alone. Ram quickly ran to find the monkey he had spoken with to try and get all the monkeys to stop harassing Computer Pirate and Hacky. Ram soon found him and explained that the pirates were only there to bury the software, not to actually steal the bananas and coconuts. The messenger monkey quickly relayed the revised message to all the monkeys who were still throwing bananas and coconuts at the pirates. They ceased throwing at once. Computer Pirate looked up at the monkeys in the tree and pleaded, "What do you want us to do? We will do anything!"

Sitting high in a banana tree hidden by all the monkeys, Ram had the perfect opportunity to ask with confidence, "How does it feel to have your treasure map stolen?"

With tears in his eyes and a little squished banana, Computer Pirate replied, "Not good at all. I am sorry for stealing copies of the software, but I never thought of it as being as valuable to Programmer as a treasure map is to a pirate. Well, this is just real bad even for a pirate to do, and I promise I will never make illegal copies again, as you monkeys are my witnesses. Hacky frantically nodded his head in agreement to what Computer Pirate was saying.

While Chip and Cam observed from a distance, Ram and the monkeys had changed the hearts of this Computer Pirates forever. They were so relieved to be free from the monkeys' mayhem, that they did not even take their dinghy, which had brought them ashore, back to the ship. They swam as fast as they could to the ship and soon were sailing away from the island. Computer Pirate and Hacky would never forget this island adventure!

As Chip and Ram walked along the beach observing the ship sail away, their attention was drawn to the pirate's dinghy. Something or someone was peeking out of the small boat. But who or what was it??

THE END

Computer Puppets Game©

Game Rules

Three players or teams select a Component. Each component or team is given 3 Brain Charge Cards

(1) **Rattle their Brains** – Ask a friend.
(2) **Brain Challenge** – Ask another component.
(3) **Brain Drain** - Ask for two multi-choice answers.

One Component spins the CD to determine who goes first. The closest Component to arrow goes first in this first spin. The Component then draws a card from top of deck. The selected Component then spins the CD to choose one of the other two Components. The selected Component has the opportunity to answer the direct question on card (no multi-choice answers should be given at this time) and answer is shown in red. If Component answers the question correctly, they keep that card. If, they cannot, the card is placed face down in the Ask a Tech stack or they may choose to use a Brain Charge Card.

The components continue until all the cards in the Question stack have been drawn. Each component then totals their cards and the component with the highest points is selected as The Tech.

The Tech picks up all cards in the Ask a Tech stack. Then they select a component of their choice to answer the multi-choice question. If chosen component cannot answer the question then the Tech gets to keep the card. When all the cards have been answered from the Tech stack, each Component will total their points. The winner is the Component with the most points.

Then a new group of two components/teams is chosen to play the winner. You play until everyone has been given a turn. You are declared the Brain if you are the winning Component of all the Games played.

Answering the questions may not be enough to win this game. Luck of the spinner and the right questions will determine if you're the winner.

Go ahead take a spin and your puppet man just might win!

*__To get all of the templates needed to make your own Computer Puppets Gameboard©
email us at computerpuppets@yahoo.com. You will be forwarded the templates via
email of all of the game pieces.__*

The Purchaser of this book should read the important information listed below about additional products and materials available to use with this instructional book:

I would like to thank you for your purchase of Volume I – Unlock Technology with the Computer Puppets for Grades 3rd –5th! The goal for this book along with the other instruction materials was created as a resource to teach a Computer 101 class that everyone can understand.

This 4–Part curriculum provides complete instructions to teach about hardware, computer programming, virus and program revisions and internet safety with fun and interactive lesson plans. The key to unlock the understanding is made possible with The Computer Puppets!

Grade level appropriate flashcards/worksheets are available to copy for the purchaser of this book. The flashcards help reinforce character or component or process recognition.

If the purchase of your book does not include the 4–Part Video Production of the Computer Puppets you may contact us at **computerpuppets@yahoo.com** for information on how to get this DVD at a minimal charge.

Last, but not least the Computer Puppets Game© templates are available free of charge via email by contacting us at **computerpuppets@yahoo.com**

Other books available soon will be:
Volume II – Unlock Technology with the
Computer Puppets for Grades K5-2nd!
Volume III – Unlock Technology with the
Computer Puppets for Preschool!

Visit us at www.computerpuppets.com

Computer Puppets Learning System

Identifying computer components and purposes.	Part I
Understanding how programs are developed.	Part II
Experiencing program revisions and viruses	Part III
Using the Internet accurately and safely	Part IV
Rainbow Pixel of Hope	Book 1
Mouse without a House	Book 2
Computer Pirates	Book 3

Key to ISTE Standards Category

Basic operations and concepts	1
Social, ethical, and human issues	2
Technology productivity tools	3
Technology communications tools	4
Technology research tools	5
Technology problem-solving and decision-making tools	6

Compton Learning Company, Inc. Profiles

Prior to completion of Grade 5, students will:	1	2	3	4	5	6	Learning System & Books
Use telecommunications efficiently to access remote information, communicate with others in support of direct and independent learning, and pursue personal interests. *Knowledge is power and The Computer Puppets is the missing link in understanding a sometimes complex computer world.*							*PARTS IV AMD BOOKS*
Use telecommunications and online resources (e.g., email, online discussions, Web environments) to participate in collaborative problem solving activities for the purpose of developing solutions or products for audiences inside and outside the classroom. *Take your abilities to new levels but learn the reason to be responsible before issues arise.*							*PARTS III, IV AND BOOKS*
Use technology resources (e.g., calculators, data collection probes, videos, educational software) for problem solving, self-directed learning, and extended learning activities. *Understand the terminology and therefore understanding directions.*							*PARTS I, II, III, IV AND BOOKS*
Determine which technology is useful and select the appropriate tools(s) and technology resources to address a variety of tasks and problems. *You can access and select your tools to accomplish the task.*							*PARTS IV AND BOOKS*
Evaluate the accuracy, relevance, appropriateness, comprehensive, and bias of electronic information sources. *The Computer Puppets will travel within the Internet and students learn the do's and don'ts first hand.*							*PART IV*

Profiles for Technology Literate Students

Prior to completion of Grade 5, students will:	1	2	3	4	5	6
Use telecommunications efficiently to access remote information, communicate with others in support of direct and independent learning, and pursue personal interests.						
Use telecommunications and online resources (e.g., email, online discussions, Web environments) to participate in collaborative problem solving activities for the purpose of developing solutions or products for audiences inside and outside the classroom.						
Use technology resources (e.g., calculators, data collection probes, videos, educational software) for problem solving, self-directed learning, and extended learning activities.						
Determine which technology is useful and select the appropriate tools(s) and technology resources to address a variety of tasks and problems.						
Evaluate the accuracy, relevance, appropriateness, comprehensive, and bias of electronic information sources.						